Eve
Use the Bathroom

Simul Iustus et Peccator
(At the Same time righteous and a sinner)

MW01165144

T. Charles Brantley

Outskirts Press, Inc.
Denver, Colorado

By Timothy C. Brantley
Pastor of Restoration Springs Inter-denominational Church
1575 Thomaston Avenue
Waterbury, CT 06704
203-753-7377
www.rest.org

Even Christians Use the Bathroom
"Simul Iustus et Peccator"

Cover Design and Illustration by samwall.com

Outskirts Press, Inc.
http://www.outskirtspress.com

ISBN: 978-1-4327-2516-7

Outskirts Press and the "OP" logo are trademarks belonging to Outskirts Press, Inc.

PRINTED IN THE UNITED STATES OF AMERICA

**THIS BOOK IS WRITTEN
FOR CHRISTIANS AND NON-CHRISTIANS**
...So Drop Your Stones

This book is dedicated to Jackie Brantley, my wife of over 22 years, and my teenagers, Timothy Charles Brantley II and Jocelyn Raquel Brantley.

This book is also in memory of the late Pastor Superintendent Charles J. Brantley of Greater Love COGIC in Tallahassee, Florida (my father, mentor, and friend).

I also thank God for my mother Ruth Brantley and my sister Michelle Brantley for their support during his passing on November 26, 2007.

This book is edited by https://www.scribendi.com.

This book has also reviewed, dissected, and analyzed by Dr. & Superintendent C. E. Richardson of Tallahassee, Florida and Superintendent Tony W. Torain of Baltimore, MD. For their protection, some and not ALL of their critiques were adhered.

I hope one day to meet and personally learn from R C Sproul Sr. and Jr., Bishop TD Jakes, Steve Brown, Bishop Eddie Long, Ravi Zacharias, Bishop Noel Jones, C J Mahaney, Bishop Blake of COGIC, Chuck Swendol, Bishop Marvin Winans, John MacArthur , Dr. Mark Dever,Dr. Myles Monroe, Dennis Rainey, Dr. W J Cambpell , Dr.David Jeremiah, Dr. Floyd Flake, Rich Warren, Dr. CornelRonald West, Michael Baisden, Steve Harvey and Tom Joyner.

Contents

Introduction.. i
Forgiveness 1
Seven Words of Christ...5
Reality Christianity 15
Some People Don't Know 19
Classic Fights 23
Simul iustus et Pecator..33
Ezekiel 16:49 49
Drop your stones John 8 63
Chief of Sinners 85
Perfect Church 89
Propitiation..97
Impute 101
Lazy – Sloths..105
If the Lord Marks 115
Romans 9:15 123
New Mercy Lamentations 3:22,23................................129
Cynics & Epicureans...133
Acts 24:16 141
Evil is Present 145

Words to Challenge..155
Accuser 162
Anger...162

Animosity...163
Assist..163
Bitterness...164
Boasting..164
Burdens...165
Comfort...166
Compassion...166
Conceited (arrogant)..167
Condemn...167
Conspire..168
Contention..168
Covetousness..169
Crafty..170
Criticize (invite demons to your house)..................171
Curse & Bless...171
Debate...172
Deceit..172
Devour...173
Disagreement..174
Disciples..174
Division (Cause It)..175
Edifying...177
Encourage..177
Enemies...178
Envying..178
Evil Speaking..179
Esteem Higher...179
Exhort..179
Family..180
Fear..180
Fighting..180
Filthy Lucre...181
Forbear..181
Forgive...182
Fraud..182
Fruit Bad..182

Fruit Good..183
Gentle..184
God Loves-We Should Love 184
Good..184
Greed...185
Grudge...186
Guile (Conspiracy, Deceit, Fraud, Hypocrisy) 186
Hate 187
Haughty...187
Honest 187
Hospitality...188
Household of Faith..188
Humble..189
Hypocrites...189
Innocent...190
Jealousy...191
Judgment 191
Keep Your Word...193
Kindness..193
Knowledge and Judgment................................194
Love in Action 195
Love in Deed..196
Love Faith 197
Love God 197
Love of God Hate Man 198
Love One Another (Royal Law) 198
Power of Love...198
Love Walk..199
Lying 200
Maliciousness...201
Marriage 201
Meek 202
Mercy 202
Murmurings..202
Neighbor 203
Offence...205

Ordination 206
Partiality..207
Peace 207
Perfectness 207
Pretence (false)..208
Pride 208
Pure Heart 209
Quarrelsome...210
Racism..211
Scorners..213
Selfish 213
Serving 213
Speak the Truth 214
Spiritual Dead 214
Strife [Competition] 214
Submit...215
Tongue 216
Truth..216
Unity 217
Unselfishness 217
Vengeance...218

Introduction

Simul Iustus et Peccator in Latin means, "at the same time righteous and a sinner." This is a famous quote from the father of the Reformation, Martin Luther. In this statement, he wanted converts to understand that even though redeemed, the sinful world still affects our lives. In essence, after conversion we still need a Savior. Because of this, the redeemed need "spiritual toilet" training.

At times, it will appear that I am talking from several sides of my mouth as it relates to Christians using the bathroom. On one term, the negative way we treat people is "using the bathroom" and on another term, the way God corrects us is 'using the Bathroom.' In addition, on another term, the evil that is within that needs to come out is 'using the bathroom.' In point, all direct to the same course of action of getting things (sins) out of us that impede our walk with the God of Abraham, Isaac, and Jacob. Going to the bathroom is healthy in our physical and "spiritual" lives. Moreover, those who hold the "waste" within will eventually destroy themselves. In direct, we all need a daily "spiritual" colon cleaning and colonoscopy.

Some Christians think once they taste the forgiveness and love of God, the work of God is done through Jesus the Christ. However, this is only the beginning of the journey and not the end. Christians must understand that after conversion, God is still working (sanctification) to get things out of us (toilet). Moreover, when we deny the toilet (sanctification),we hurt ourselves. A Christian will not lay aside the weight because they will deny or cover the weight (Hebrews12:1). However, when a Christian goes to the bathroom (sanctification) one is relieved daily of the sins and walks just a little closure to the savior.

In understanding that we have sin within after conversation to Christ, we would be more inclined to judge ourselves than others solely. Our love for God and His creatures would go to another level. The power of judging another brother or sister says the same why I judge and pass down punishment on another brother is the same way the judgment will come upon me (Matthews 7). This means that if I judge harshly and without grace, God will measure me with the same harshness.

How changed would the body of Christ be if we adhered? Reaping does not just refer to money, but also to the love and time that I give to somebody else. Let us be truthful: there are people within the body of Christ that we just cannot stand.

We shout and scream with them during the church service but after that, all we want is to get as far away. We live in this reality.

The reality is that I can love the person in Christ but I cannot stand their personality in day-to-day life. Yet this is where the power of God comes into my reality. It is through the dying of the self that I can gain the glory of God.

There can be no healing unless there is an admission of the problem. Until we admit to ourselves that we are guilty, the Lord cannot take us to the next level. The next level is saying "God help me to love my brother in Christ on a continuing basis".

If one rumor needs to be killed, it is the rumor that loving everybody is easy. This is not the case. In essence, we must remember that the first murder was not between strangers but between brothers. Not much has changed over the years.

This hatred and indifference keeps Christians from talking to one another on a continuing basis. The truth of Christianity is that there are many different opinions of the Bible and doctrine that are taught. How else can you explain the many denominations in the world today?

It is only recently that different denominations have finally matured and started to talk. Even with this new dialog, however, we still continue to hurt one another while the devil sits back and says thank you for doing his job. This cloud of pain deflects us from the essence of the gospel, which is to love.

I'll reiterate: the essence of the gospel is not to be rich or famous, it is to love. If we do not love, we are going to be in trouble. It can be hard to love all people but this is the commandment of our savior. Love is what Jesus is. Love starts at home. When we do not love, we make His death and resurrection meaningless.

This is why we as Christians must tell the world that we are not perfect. God is working on us. Yes, we sit on the toilet like everybody else. In addition, usually our spiritual toilet actions are manifest in how we deal with other personalities.

God saves, but personalities remain the same. They are always there and they do not always mesh. What God does is add spiritual points to your personality so you have the strength to do the right thing at the right time.

This book is titled "Even Christians Use the Bathroom" because I want Christians to know that we are not perfect. I think every Christian knows this but sometimes we do not act like it. In fact, we sometimes walk around like Pharisee peacocks.

We are not saved to impress each other. We are saved to reach a dying and lost generation. Nothing will ever change that. We are who we are by His grace and His grace alone.

We must walk with a billboard to a dying world that says, "Yes, if Jesus can save me, He can save you too."

We all have character flaws. We all have things in our lives that we do not like. There are issues that hinder our progress in one way or another. This book will open our eyes to see our flaws first before we see those of others. It is important that we see our sins more than others do.

In these examinations of ourselves, we must distinguish between sinful and adiaphorous actions. For too long the church has called things sinful when in reality they are not sinful but adiaphorous; neither bad nor good.

This is especially true in the Pentecostal church. In addition, while things un-sinful have been called sinful, we have lost a generation of people who got dislocated from the entire event because we pressed them to stop things that were not sinful at all.

In reality, we put heavy loads on people when we cannot carry them ourselves. In fact, it is the same people who are so stuck in reality that became crazy or left the faith. To me, this is not telling the world you have flaws in your own life. We must undo such actions and show people Christ, not our own great works of salvation.

This is why we must realize that in spite of our flaws and sins, we are still useful to the Lord. We must shout this out. As lustful as Samson was, his hair grew back. Well, if Samson can be useful, so can we. We cannot hold this truth to ourselves, however; we must prorogate this message to all.

In simple points, we are sinners saved by grace. This book will cover several points. On **one** hand, we are on the toilet because God is <u>working on us to get sins out of us</u>. **Secondly**, we must <u>admit "I am on the toilet"</u>. **Thirdly**, we must <u>admit that things that come out of us that are not pleasing to God,</u> including hate and bitterness. **Fourthly,** and most importantly, we must tell the world that we are on the toilet and <u>we are not perfect but</u> we are what we are by His grace and mercy alone.

He is working on me continually. He is working out of me so that I can see my savior all the better. He is getting things out me so that the world can see the light of Christ in me. He is working on me so that I can recognize that I cannot live without Him, because I am constantly subject to my sinful nature.

Sin is sin. There is not one sin worse than another. All require judgment. All require Hell. This is especially true for believers, not because we know better but because of our self-righteousness; we think we are better than others. No sir or madam—all have sinned and come short of His glory. Yes, Christian brother and sister, that includes you.

God is constantly working on us. He is constantly working things out of us. Only a fool walks around as if they have it all worked out. No, we do not have it worked out. We are always being worked on for His glory.

This book will challenge all to work on those non-popular points in the word of God. At the end of this book, there is a list of verses that will hopeful challenge our walk with the Lord.

Forgiveness

An exercise that must be completed on a daily basis is to forgive those who have wronged us. In conjunction with Bible study, prayer, fasting and good deeds, we all need to put forgiveness in our daily spiritual diet. Without it, the excess fat of the flesh will be heavy upon us.

As Christians, we can say all the good words and deeds that we like, but if we cannot forgive a brother for the wrong that he or she has committed against us, we cannot be forgiven for our sins. Forgiving is hard but necessary.

At times I have prayed to God to have one ask me for my forgiveness, but after understanding the scriptures I realized that I needed to forgive others, whether they ask for forgiveness or not. This is a true test of Christianity; it is the test of laying down your personal feelings so that you can clear the air.

In Matthew 5, we are given the road map for this act. In essence, the scripture points out that it is good to have a gift at the altar, but if that gift does not include forgiveness, the

Word of the Lord says to drop everything and clear things with thy brother and then return to offer the gift.

Christianity, at times, has promoted just the opposite. I have kept on giving my gift while hating a brother. I have kept on preaching as a pastor even though I envied another brother or sister in Christ. However, true Christianity includes letting things go.

This is the meaning of the word of God. There is no second interpretation of it. If we have a problem with somebody, we must clear it up. Yet over time, people have justified their hate, bitterness and envy through the equivocation of this scripture.

Not letting things go will prepare you for falls in your flesh. By letting things go, you in essence hold on to the hand of God versus the hand of the one who has offended. In so many points, Christ could have been hard on those that physically abused Him, but he was not. This is the lesson that we must pray to learn.

Until we learn to be like Steven, who prayed and forgave people while they killed him, we are heading for a fall within our own lives. Unless we can forgive while they crucify us, we can never see the Kingdom of Heaven in our own lives.

Is this easy? Of course not. However, it takes us to a point of power and strength because we finally learn how to tap into the realm of God's love. This is a goal of greatness. Tapping into my own flesh and my own level of love and forgiveness will keep me within a certain border. However, if we tap and hit the love and grace of God then we prepare ourselves to walk in his glory. We can do all the religious stuff but if we cannot forgive and love our brothers, we are headed for a great fall.

The true grace of God is not grace until you pass it to some body else. You may speak like the angels but if you do not exhibit charity, it profits nothing. Again, it is forgiving your brother & sister without them asking for forgiveness first. In addition, you do this not when you feel like it but every day of your life.

We cannot forget *Ex nihilo nihil fit*, which means from nothing comes nothing. This phrase came from Parmenides. The point is that if we have nothing to give, how can we expect to get anything back?

Too many Christians are shouting and praising God without giving anything to their fellow man. Christ has given us all, so in return we should give all to keep the unity of the body. However, because of our old mind frames we have not been released. Hence, Christians use the bathroom. It's one thing to destroy a stranger's bathroom but to destroy a brother's bathroom is even worse. We must make changes in this matter. Until we can pass on the forgiveness that we have received by the grace of God, we will not go forward.

Seven Words Of Christ

As we look at the last seven words of Christ, we see a pattern of talking to God, man and both. Three times, He refers to God. Two times, He refers to humankind. Two times, He refers to both. As we look at His death words, we should let them become life words resonant in our spiritual bones.

Luke 23:34 *(Talking to God)*
Then said Jesus, Father, forgive them; for they know not what they do. In addition, they parted his raiment, and cast lots.

The first thing Christ gave as He died was forgiveness to his enemies. The passion with which He gave the statement was powerful within itself because it was not given after the fact but DURING the pain and anguish.

There was no time lapse—He was able to let go of the pain and accept the grace that the living God gave unto him. Help us all to not put a timetable on people because of the

5

offences that we feel have been dealt by others. The struggle is not just forgiving but doing it without your enemies' asking.

In our pride, we want our enemies to come and ask for forgiveness. This was not the case with Christ. He gave without his enemies asking. This is a statement of greatness that we all must try to attain. Greatness not in money, fame or fortune, but greatness in letting go and touching the heart of God by dealing charitably with our brothers.

We have been spoiled by watered down gospel that has made us feel that we are owed the power of Christ's blood. However, we are not owed the grace and love that God has given to us. It is *Extra Nos* or outside of us. The way God has dwelt with us is nothing of our own doing but comes from outside of us.

I do not believe in UFOs but if we consider *Extra Nos* as a noun, it becomes clear that we might believe in them because the way God deals with us is outside of our own understanding and learning. However, the point is not just to receive God's love but to share it with others. Therefore, as Christ gave us grace we need to do the same unto others.

In other words, His enemies were not even paying attention to the grace that He was extending to them. This sounds so familiar because there are times that we forgive and the ones who have wronged us go right on inflicting the wrongs. What we must remember is that it isn't about what other people do, it's about what we do.

Can we take up this cross and carry it to the end or will we drop the ball?

We all need the power to let go while the person who is the source of our pain continues to work on us. Christ talks to God first because it takes God to provide the strength to let go and forgive. One cannot do it by their own power. God must supply the fuel to create forgiveness. As Christians, we say it pains us but we MUST also let go of the pain. we admit we are on the toilet by saying we are hurt, yet by passing this pain on, we are able to love in spite of it.

Matthew 27:46 *(Talking to God)*
In addition, about the ninth hour Jesus cried with a loud voice, saying, Eli, Eli, lama sabachthani? That is to say, My God, my God, why hast thou forsaken me?

We see Christ talking to His Father. As Christ talked to the Father while in distress, so should we cry out to the Father when it is hard to do the things that he wants us to do.

We as Christians may feel abandoned because we see God calling for us to do much while others do nothing at all. But we must understand that the Lord may use others to show us the light. As Joseph saw the hand of God through his wicked brothers, so should we see it through our enemies. Joseph did not respond with evil, he responded with love. This book is meant to be a challenge; testing our walk with God.

We want to respond when people do us wrong but our

7

conversation should not be with people but with God Himself. It takes a high degree of suffering to attain the spiritual awareness to call on God and we must struggle to leave the constraints of our minds and catch Christ. On the cross, he gave us a perfect example. While being hit and misunderstood, we should not hold back love. This is the toilet issue of life. I must go against what I do not want to do. Paul had to struggle to do right and so do we.

John 19:26-27 *(Talking to Man)*

When Jesus therefore saw his mother, and the disciple standing by, whom he loved, he saith unto his mother, Woman, behold thy son!

Then saith He to the disciple, Behold thy mother! In addition, from that hour that disciple took her unto his own home.

We see the love of Jesus toward his mother. We learn here the power of loving and becorned by others even when you are having problems. It is always easy for us to go into our turtle shells when problems come, but we learn from Christ to come out of that shell and love anyway.

In fact, when we learn to focus on love instead of pain we are able to triumph. I say to all who read this; we must continue the battle within. We must fight the good fight of faith. The biggest and most important fights are within, not without.

I hope that this book can help others to see that not every fight is of the devil; some are from God to help us reach higher ground. Yet while we go through the tests of life, we must not become bitter, we must become better as our Lord and Savior teaches.

John 19:28 *(Talking to Both God and Man)*
After this, Jesus knowing that all things were now accomplished, that the scripture might be fulfilled, saith, I thirst.

What we learn from this scripture is the power of being honest. The son of God is telling all that he is having a flesh issue. We as Christians must learn to tell others in the spirit of love what is bothering us. We must tell the world that we are not perfect. The perfection movement does not work. Only standing at the foot of the cross will lead to our salvation.

Justification is instant but sanctification is a process in our lives. We have flesh that works on our minds. I agree with what John Macarthur said: "And we are constantly battling the mind to do what is right." This is why we must try to learn to be honest about our sins and seek ways to demonstrate the love of God to others every day.

When we hold back love, we lose an opportunity to have the Spirit come in and bring unity among disunity. Many become super apostles (2 Corinthians) and act like nothing bothers them, but we forget we are still on the toilet. We are still in this FLESH suit. When we are faced with a problem, we must DEAL and not run from it.

Rather, we must run to the problems in our lives. We as Christians do not like to have confrontations. There is no sin in comforting in love. However, there is sin when we do not confront those that are hurting us, especially when we have an issue against another.

We must understand that sometimes things can get messy when we deal with problems, but they still must be dealt with. We cannot run from such issues in life. We must deal with the elephant that is in the room—the elephant is not going anywhere on its own.

So, as in the toilet, things may get messy but must be done. So can talking to a Christian about issues become messy. If you hurt or thirst, you must speak of it and let the chips fall at the cross of Christ. You must admit the pain in order to get past it, push it back as did Christ, and find another way to live.

Luke 23:43 *(Talking to Man)*
In addition, Jesus said unto him, Verily I say unto thee, today shalt thou be with me in paradise.

Here Christ talks to an ungodly man. Jesus could have been self-righteous but he was more loving than condemning. What can we learn from this?

We know how to launch back and hurt others when we are hurt but Christ gives us an example and tells a sinner: you will be with me in paradise.

Why have we Christians always got to go into a hole and hide from the world when things happen? We must change this habit and say to others, "We are human beings, all made in the image of God. Since we are His image, we cannot look down on one another."

God forgive us for looking down on others. God forgive us for being guilty of James 2 and beating up others who do not have what we have.

We must move away from this notion that we are better than others. All are at the foot of the cross. Only God picks whom He desires, by the spirit and not the deeds. This is according to the gospel of John. Since this is true, how dare I put another down?

We all are on the toilet. How dare we condemn without first looking at ourselves? We all must change that ungodly attitude. Yes, Jesus saw the sin but he also saw the pain in this bother. We as Christians have not learned to have mercy on others. We know how to judge. We justify our own sins but condemn others. We must stop this foolishness. Jesus saw and had compassion. We must walk in the same path of righteousness. We must look at others as Christ looks at us—not in judgment but in love. Is there judgment? Yes, but there is also a God who wants us to treat each other as he treats us all.

John 19:30 *(Talking to God & Man)*
When Jesus therefore had received the vinegar, he said, it is finished: and he bowed his head, and gave up the ghost.

God is always working on us, especially as we deal with our fellow man. What I am trying to relate is that life is a process. We cannot stand up and say, "I am done and complete". We cannot declare to the world that we cannot improve. Only God has that distinction on judgment day when He says we are well done or finished.

Therefore, Christian brothers or sisters get use to the crapper. God is always working on us. We will stay on the potter's wheel. One may not be entangled in the same sin, but all is still sin in God's eyes.

In addition, it is harmful to claim that we can reach perfection because men and women have walked away with messed up mentalities from trying to achieve something that they can never reach on their own. Only God sanctifies, not man.

Again, when we claim we are finished we forget that we are still on the toilet. In fact saying you are finished growing is immature. Only God knows who and what we are. Man does not have the power. Do you remember when the disciples were mad at James and John for wanting to be number one? Well, that is the same thing as Christians saying they have all the answers.

In my mind, this points straight for a Gnostic mind frame. Gaining more knowledge (Gnostic) is not the answer. In me dwells no good thing. This is truth and scripture. We have nothing good in ourselves alone, but in Christ, we find redemption and atonement. At one moment, we are set free.

Luke 23:46 *(Talking to God)*
In addition, when Jesus cried with a loud voice,

12

he said, Father, into thy hands I commend my spirit: and having said thus, he gave up the ghost.

The only way we can grow in grace is to commend all to God. Commend dealing with our brothers. Commend loving our wives. Commend all our sins and issues to God. When you do not do this, you miss a great miracle. That miracle is loving the unlovable.

We all have experienced the unlovable. It is a necessary part of being blessed. While in the bathroom, we must let the world know that we are doing this not because of our own power but because of the power of God in our lives. We must let the world know that it is not our power but His. We have commended our lives to God and expect God to do those things that we cannot do on our own.

We cannot live this life on our own. We cannot judge others without first judging ourselves. How dare we point at people for their faults without talking about our own? This is not commending our spirit.

We must embrace the spirit of knowing how to judge others. We must put down our stones. We cannot continue to point at others with no love in our hearts. How dare we look at others and paint them as no good when without God's grace we would be nothing?

This is the essence of this book. We must commend our spirits. We must commend our attitudes. We must commend our dreams to God so that he can take the glory. All glory to the Father and none to me.

Reality Christianity

The point of the matter is that at times Christians may lose the essence of why Christ came to die for their sins. He did not come so that we could show off in religious circles. He came that we might have life and abundance in that life. The key is that before and during salvation, Christ must take the throne—there is no sharing.

However, in some climates it has been subconsciously given that we need only knowledge and no longer God. However, I beg to differ; we are in this flesh suit and will never get to the point where we do not need God in and through our lives.

Which brings me to the point of understanding that since we live in this suit of flesh, we will have shortcomings, but to not share them with the world is the greatest shortcoming of all. That is because in not telling the world of our shortcomings, we give the world a false idea that Christians are perfect. We give the world a false sense of hope; a hope that is not built on Christ but on us.

When we tell the world that we are perfect, we fail to take others to the cross and we share a lying tongue that we have arrived. We have not arrived—we have ALL just started this journey.

The word 'perfect' in the Bible is translated as complete. To be honest, we never want to get to a point in our lives that we do not need God any more. We want him ALWAYS shaping and molding us into the person He needs us to be. We never want to get to a point where we tell God "You can stop working on me NOW because I got myself together." This is a dangerous point to live in. In fact, if he is done you are grave yard dead.

I am a sinner saved by grace. This message does not help anybody until it is shared with somebody else. However, there are times when we as Christians walk around as if we never go the bathroom. In other words, we act like we are spiritual super-humans and nothing can touch or bother us. I beg to differ. If you kick me I will feel it like any sinner would, the only difference is I take my self to the altar and ask God to wipe me clean.

This is why God's grace is new every morning. It is why my place in God is renewed by his grace every day, it is why we as Christians must tell the world about this grace that blesses our lives.

If we do not tell them than we are nothing but agents of Satan, who live and breathe lies. We have to stop lying to the world in telling them with our actions and self-righteousness that we have no problems. Learn to accept not only your faults but also the faults of others. May he who is without sin cast the first stone.

We as Christians wake up and thank God for his grace. Our marriages, jobs, children, and churches all have problems but we just take our problems to God in prayer. We take our habits to God in prayer. From there He gives us divine steps and orders to help us deal with the different points of pain within our lives.

We cannot forget that power is perfected in weakness. This is a quote from John Macarthur: "For this to be true, we must confess our weakness not only to Christians but also to a point to non-believers."

I cannot tell you how many people have said to me that they would not come to the church because they are afraid of the church falling down on them. Why do people have this issue? I believe this is due do the mind frame that Christians are perfect and because they are not they cannot come in.

We have to change this notion. We have to change this false doctrine. As Paul had false doctrine in his day, we have the same issues in our day as well. We have those that say unless you are perfect and totally healed, you are not a Christian. This is not correct in any way. We must follow sound doctrine. Christ is alive and well but we cannot and will never take His place. He is the only perfect person. We are not perfect.

Dr. Sproul says that a point that many people do not get is that Christ was perfect while on this Earth. It seems many people are staking a claim to that distinction. Yet, no one can claim that. Christ alone takes away the sins of the world. This again is why we must let the world know that we Christians do not have our stones all in a row. If we did, why would we need grace every morning?

Christians, tell the world that you still use the toilet of life. We press on despite faults and sins by His grace and not our own. Let us keep the gospel real as Christ did. Even Jesus sat with sinners. So why do Christians segregate themselves from others? I know the Bible speaks of coming out from among them and being separate, but there is a balance because Christ calls us the salt of the earth.

Again, Jesus spoke to the sinners, so what is our problem and issue within our lives? Speak and live the truth. Jesus hung around sinners so much that they called him a sinner. The world has gotten into reality TV so its time for the church to do the same. Take off the mask and tell the world that it is Christ that does the work and not Christians.

We cannot continue to wear the mask of righteousness. We cannot continue a front that is so ungodly. We are sinners who are saved by grace. No works or merit can measure up to the work of Christ upon our lives. We must let the world know that God is working on us full time. In so doing, we can reach the lost not by words but by the examples that God gives to us.

Some People
Just Don't Know

If you do not share your feelings, those around you may never know the pain that you carry due to their non-diligence. Imagine hurting someone and not really knowing it, and then learning that the other persons swears you did know and did it on purpose.

A revelation God gave me was that there are people who hold negative opinions about another person without telling the other person how they feel. Let us all be honest. There are times when our emotions get the best of us and our imaginations play games on us. In other words, we are sometimes angry with people who are unaware of our feelings. This is Satan trying to have brothers and sisters fight against one another.

You cannot have a fight unless your opponent knows he is in the boxing ring with you. This is the same for spiritual struggles. Hitting, boxing, and cutting another brother when he does not know there is a problem is not only a waste of time, but it gives the enemy a foothold that can cause problems in the end.

In ALL points if we confront our brother in the spirit of love, our lives would be radically different than they are when we do not. Remember that the devil is the GREAT accuser of the brethren and he will do anything to distract our attention away from God and onto the pain caused by our fellow man. Your hope and focus should be on God and not the pain. Focusing on pain will never allow the healing process to begin.

Once again, this helps us to tell the truth. No one likes conformation, but sometimes it is necessary to talk through problems and clear the air. This part of the book is given because when you do not comfort others for things they have done, you will quickly become bitter. Your relationship with that person will move from a stage of harmless annoyance to a stage of disrepair.

When we find that fault, we must work it out quickly. We must not allow Satan to dig a deeper foundation. Remember, we are on the toilet. There is no way we can go through life without some form of hurt.

Life cuts. Life hurts in ways we never imagined. We take these issues to Christ but we must also let the world know that we do have struggles. We do have sin. And we must tell the world that God does not answer every prayer in the ways we expect.

When wounded, I must tell the other person in love what he or she have done. When you tell them in love, you have the power of God in your life; you are able to take a higher position.

Yet if we do not confess our faults to each other then we are again missing an opportunity to reach the lost in a special way. We are missing an opportunity to take people from pain to gain. We are missing an opportunity to show people that yes, we may have pain but we move on.

We need more inspiring testimonies. The world claps when they see a hurt person move on. Where are the inspiring persons in the body of Christ? It seems all is well. No pain, no hurt, no ill will, no inspiration. We must turn and stop this mess. We are all brokers who have been hurt by the cares of this world, but we press on. This is what the world needs to hear. These similar words inspired Paul, who inspired generations. We need to do the same thing.

Christians, talk about your bad marriages, difficult children, tedious job, your church and your lives. Let the world see your scars and let them applaud for the glory of God in your lives. Let them see us disagree and yet still love one another and not tear each other down.

There must be a **congruence** of spirit within our churches. There must be a congruence of spirit in our jobs. However, we have to be honest about the issues and pressure that hit all of us. Only when we are able to fight such things can we find peace.

Sometimes the peace is not what God gives freely, but what we strive for. The Bible says as much; it is within your reach to be at peace with your brother and sisters. We have to show others both sides of the coin. When we can show both sides, souls will come running to Christ.

We tell people that once they are saved, all problems will go away. No sir, Christ came not to solve problems but to save so that we can experience fellowship with one with another. Let them see our tears and difficulties and in return, they will embrace Christ.

Classic Fights in Biblical Times

Throughout the Bible, there are classic fights between brothers that help us to learn not to let the enemy Satan create a foothold between ourselves and a co-worker or family member. Yes, we are sinners, but we should use the power of God to help fight back bitterness.

Cain and Abel

The first murder was committed by a brother who has jealous of his brother. Envy, strife, and other things ruled the mind of Cain to the point that when God gave him a means of escape he denied it. Cain denied it to the point that he murdered his brother.

Murder can be perpetrated in several ways. Murder is not just physical, but can be emotional too. You can also spiritually murder someone. The tongue can be either a dagger or a tool of encouragement. You decide which.

What makes the point of Cain and Abel so powerful is that Cain killed his brother because of the style of worship. He did it because the Lord accepted Abel's and not Cain's sacrifice (worship), and when God corrected Cain, he turned around and killed his brother.

Not much has changed. When the Lord convicts us do we go and find a brother to murder or do we say it is me O Lord standing in need of prayer?

Cain killed. How many bodies are around us slain by our criticism towards one another? How many have stopped coming to church due to our negative comments? The key to understanding the story of Cain and Abel is taking the correction and moving on.

It is important to note that the first murder was not between strangers but between brothers. There is something to be said about that. The ones who we may kill may be brothers or sisters instead of the accuser of the brethren.

This is important because it gives us the truth that sexual sin is not the only sin. We really see the sin of covetousness at work on Cain. Because Abel trusted his brother, he walked with his brother to his own death. In no way did Abel imagine his brother killing him. In no way did he think Cain was capable of murder. Well, we must be careful of the same. The sin of Cain lives on in every believer.

There is no way we can expect God to move when we beat one another up. How can we reach the world when we cannot even reach our own brothers? We have been fooling ourselves in believing that as long as our gift is flowing we are all right. If we murder our brother or sister in word or deed, then we are guilty.

I know that what I say in this book may get me *Exsurge Domine*. In other words, many may shun me and not want fellowship with me because my words take them away from a self-serving motif that has entered the land.

Martin Luther heard *Exsurge Domine* in 1520 from Pope Leo X. In no way do I compare myself to Martin Luther. But there must be an outcry from all believers. That outcry is that God alone and not man but God alone .

For reasons of wealth, we have forgotten why we are here. We are here to show and demonstrate the glory and love of God to the world and to each other. However, many souls have been lost to the false paradigm of a prosperity & perfect mind-frame church. We must first remind ourselves that we are not perfect. We must take off the mask and tell the world that we all have problems within our churches, but that Christ is still in love with his church and is looking for us to make changes in our lives.

Oh, church of God I am making a clarion call for all to put down their sticks and stones toward one another. I encourage all to examine one self and see how one has hurt brothers and why such has occurred. Last I read one should restore a brother and not destroy a brother (Galatians 6).

By the way, some interact, like pirates. There are Christian pirates who take from others for the sake of their OWN personal kingdom. Please remember that the crusaders wore crosses on their battle amour, raped, and killed for the cause of Jerusalem. We must be careful of this righteousness trap.

ANYBODY can call himself or herself Christians. Anyone can put God on any door and call it a church. Ones proclamation ALONE does not make them a Christian. Your walk with God and man through Jesus the Christ is a key component. Furthermore, your humble spirit of your faults and sins is another ingredient of your profession of your faith.

If we could see ourselves as being on the toilet, we would spend less time killing and more time loving. We would make opportunities to love rather than hate. We would take the opportunity to restore rather than bury.

The world is watching us. They are taking notes of how we treat one another. We all must do better in the house of God. We tell the world to come into our churches for salvation, but in the meantime, there is fighting and kicking within. Yes, we have to show the power of God through how we treat one another in life and passion. They will know us not by our churches or congregation but by our love for one another.

We must stop the violence. We must stop the Christian-on-Christian crime. In doing such, we will cause the world to look at our savior and see how he has changed our lives for his glory and honor.

Joseph & Brothers

This is the classic story of jealousy and forgiveness that we all need to learn. Despite the bad way Joseph's brothers treated him, Joseph forgave them. He had every right to strike back but instead he loved. During and after his father's life, Joseph saw the good born from the bad his brothers had done. How many times do we focus on pain to the degree that we can see nothing else in our lives?

Each one of us must make a decision whether to act in love or live in hate. Yes, this problem is among Christians. Can you imagine how Christians say they love the Lord but cannot stand another Christian? There is something wrong with this picture. We cannot continue to justify such feelings and actions.

This is a prime example of being on the toilet. We shout, sing, preach and shout around it but we still hate and plot against one another. This is the work of the devil. And it is happening every day.

This hate thing is an emotional cancer that attacks our spiritual being. We must decide to love and love consistently. When we do not love, we are no better than a murderer. When we do not love, we are no better than a chief sinner.

Hear me, Christian. Hear me, Christian celebrity. When you hate and jump on people without love and mercy, you are no better than the one you attack. This again is why I write this book. We Christians have wrinkles among us.

The biggest wrinkle is how we handle and deal with one another.

Grace must be shared and not bottled up. Joseph saw the grace that God gave him during the years he was in Egypt. Because he recognized it, he also gave it to his brothers. This is a very powerful point. Joseph could have killed but he gave grace. Joseph could have slandered but he gave grace. Joseph could have murdered but he gave grace instead.

Have we gotten pain and given back pain? Have we received dishonesty and given back dishonesty? We know how to recognize and give pain. However, if we are going to be great Christians we must get beyond ourselves and see the love of God that has been given to us.

We allow pirates and cannibals in our pulpits, all for the sake of having greater numbers. However, what is the cost? We Christians sit on the toilet when we do not love and appreciate one another. We are in the bathroom when we covet and commit piracy against one another's congregation.

Another point is that Joseph forgave his brothers during life. He did not wait until they died; he forgave them on the spot. We must ask ourselves, do we wait when people come to us or do we forgive quickly? What is growing in our garden? People can plant but it is up to us to nurture growth. This is a point that you must **ANSWER**.

David & Saul

The relationship between David and Saul is classic. Saul is a king who should have helped this young man get ready for the kingdom, but instead he tried to kill David. In addition, when David had the advantage over Saul, he did not kill him. Instead, he loved him. He forgave him. He gave him another chance, which Saul did not take advantage of.

This book is written is to help fight the devouring spirit that has crept into the house of God. People have taken to anointing over loving. However, the Bible says in 1 Corinthians chapter 13 that love is more important than anything else in life.

Yes, the world needs to know that people in the church are killing one another. There are drive by killings every Sunday and church night as fellow Christians attack one another for the sake of nothing concrete.

We all need to take a page from Brother David and forgive our Sauls. There are not enough pages of this book to contain all the mentors who have killed their apprentice for the sake of envy. There are many hurt people in the body of Christ because one did not truly have love for another. Truly, this messy stuff happens in our church.

I must take a break to say that due to my own actions, I have hurt many of people. I write to help other pastors to not fall into the same hole that I have fallen into repeatedly. This book does not just cover the church but family as well.

We all need to clean up of these types of injuries on the body of Christ. If we wound everybody around us, who is left to encourage and attend to our wounds?

David had to take the steps of change. Many times, we wait for others to make the moves, but David teaches us to make the first move. If we are going to be great, some one will have to make the best and first move in love of the Lord.

Together we stand and divided we fall into Satan's power and might. Yes, we have to make changes and be honest with others and ourselves.

Paul and Barnabas

Acts 15 verse 39 records a power plot that occurred between two friends. Yes, church folks can and will fight. Paul the apostle is known for traveling around the world. He is known for writing most of the New Testament. But Paul had a mean frame of mind.

I know many people do not want to identify with Paul because he got so upset with Barnabas that they went their separate ways. This is an issue that happens within the church every day. The key is not to have contentions but to make up and fight the enemy together and not from opposite sides.

Yes, the apostle lost it with Barnabas. They got so angry that they were rent asunder. The word asunder in the Greek is ap-okh-o-rid-zo. This means to rend apart. Yes, people in the church have gotten so into their own agendas that they have forgotten about God's agenda.

We can easily forget that God wants us to do His will when we are distracted by our own. Yet because some Christians have forgotten their place relative to the savior, they have lost the true vision of the church. The vision of the church is not to increase numbers, it is to preach the word of God.

It has never been about opinion. Paul had a big fight and could have killed Mark, but in the end, Paul called Mark back for help. We must all understand ourselves and not beat one another up.

Many have stayed away from the church because of the words of a fellow Christian. We might say that Christians have killed more Christians than non-Christians. We talk about martyrs but some Christians have emotionally killed each other more than non-Christians have. We must really examine ourselves to ensure we are not fighting and rebuking another Christian beyond repair. Yes, there will be disagreements but not to the point of emotional murder. We have to remember that we are serving the same God.

We all must let the spirit of God move these emotional tendencies out of us. Yes, we are surly on the crapper to get all sins out of us. Yes, Christ redeems us once we accept His plan, but in us remains evil and pain. As Christians, we must recognize this paradigm of redemption and sin. Yet due to this paradigm, we have Ephesians 5:26 that states the WORD (Bible or Logos) washes and cleanses (Christians using the bathroom) us from the sins of life.

I hope this brief example of Christians fighting will help us to not repeat our mistakes. While we fight, there are souls to be saved. While we are at one another's throats, we are failing to see the bigger picture, which is Christ and Christ alone.

In the words of a great theologian, Frederick Buechner: *"Your life and my life flow into each other as wave flows into wave, and unless there is peace and joy and freedom for you, there can be no real peace or joy or freedom for me. To see reality--not as we expect it to be but as it is--is to see that unless we live for each other and in and through each other, we do not really live very satisfactorily; that there can really be life only where there really is, in just this sense, love."*

This quote to me is the essence of how we should behave toward one another. As I have asked again and again; how can we reach the world when they see us crapping, vomiting, and fighting one another for a special seat? They see our numbers more than our love. They see our churches more than our faithfulness to the word of God.

I must relate to my brother; I cannot have a disdain for him because God blesses him. Hatred must be repelled. When we hate, despise, and fail to pray for another we are guilty of emotional murder. Last I read, all murderers will have their place in the Lake of Fire.

Sinner and Saint

It is truly mysterious that though we are predestined, we are still sinners. This is the essence of the message of Martin Luther upon the breakout of the Reformation. His statement was given because of man's total depravity. In other words, we are not savable by our own hand even after conversion. There is no way that man in his fallen state has the power to lift himself up.

When Adam sinned, he spread a virus called sin. The allegory of sin is falling into a well that is so deep one need a savior. We are in the well and it took the hand of God Almighty to draw us out. And by Christ's death, burial and resurrection the payment of sin has been FULLY satisfied.

For explanation, we look to the Old Testament and the story of the scapegoat. In this practice, the high priest or representative of God would lay hands on two goats. In the laying on of hands one goat was killed for the sin but the other was let go because the sin was transferred. The same thing happened when Jesus and Barrabos stood before Pilate. Barrabos was let go but Jesus was killed. My point is that the sin was never wiped clean, it was given to another. That other was Jesus the Christ.

The Roman custom was an acquittal before either trial or pardon of the condemned. In the point of Barabbos, this was a pardon of the condemned. Many feel we are acquitted which means there is no crime—as if the crime never happened.

However, we as Christians cannot twist or confuse a pardon with an acquittal. The sin is still there but the power of God cries out pardon. We see the sin but we refuse to give justice. Instead of justice, we give judgment. But that not the way of Christ.

This is why Luther called us saint and sinner. Not to sin more but to recognize that we are what we are but by the grace and mercy of God. We deserve judgment but he gives us mercy. Do not ever confuse the two. Do not believe that you are all that.

Again, we stand condemned. Condemned means judgment has been passed. The judge has given the gavel and pronounced us guilty. This is the power of the blood. It overcomes our guilt. As bad as our sins are, the blood covers. Thank God, it covers us. It says to the Father "do not kill but let him live not like a condemned sinner but as a resurrected son".

As Frederick the Wise protected Martin Luther through the Reformation, the blood of Jesus covers us from all of our sins. Without Frederick, there might not have been a Reformation. Without Christ's death, burial and resurrection we would not have life external for those called by God.

John (1:29) says, "The next day John seeth Jesus coming unto him, and saith, Behold the Lamb of God, which taketh away the sin of the world." The phrase 'taketh away' means to carry the sins of the world. Sin is not erased it is taken away. It was taken from us unto Christ.

This is powerful and humbling us to know. Isaiah (53:11) says "He shall see of the travail of his soul, and shall be satisfied: by his knowledge shall my righteous servant justify many; for he shall bear their iniquities".

Notice how God said bear their sins. This again points to the power of Christ, not just in bearing our sins but the sins of all who would believe.

The following scriptures emphasize this point:

Exodus (28:38) And it shall be upon Aaron's forehead, that Aaron may bear the iniquity of the holy things, which the children of Israel shall hallow in all their holy gifts; and it shall be always upon his forehead, that they may be.

Leviticus (16:21) And Aaron shall lay both his hands upon the head of the live goat, and confess over him all the iniquities of the children of Israel, and all their transgressions in all their sins, putting them upon the head of the goat, and them upon the head of the goat, and shall send him away by the hand of a fit man into the wilderness:

(16:22) And the goat shall bear upon him all their iniquities unto a land not inhabited: and he shall let go the goat in the wilderness.

Numbers (18:1) And the LORD said unto Aaron, Thou and thy sons and thy father's house with thee shall bear the iniquity of the sanctuary: and thou and thy sons with thee shall bear the iniquity of your priesthood.

Hebrews (9:28) So Christ was once offered to bear the sins of many; and unto them that look for him shall he appear the second time without sin unto salvation.

Romans (5:15) But not as the offence, so also is the gift. For if through the offence of one many be dead, much more the grace of God, and the gift by grace, which is by one man, Jesus Christ, hath abounded unto many.

2 Corinthians (5:21) For he hath made him to be sin for us, who knew no sin; that we might be made the righteousness of God in him.

Leviticus (10:17) Wherefore have ye not eaten the sin offering in the holy place, seeing it is most holy, and God hath given it you to bear the iniquity of the congregation, to make atonement for them before the LORD?

Galatians (3:13) Christ hath redeemed us from the curse of the law, being made a curse for us: for it is written, Cursed is every one that hangeth on a tree.

These are only a few scriptures that express the depravity of man and how Christ took on the sins of the world. When we act as if we have no sin we negate the work of

Christ. To me that is blasphemy.

People want reality and not falsehood. They want to know that God will use them as they are. Yes, we are justified quickly but the work of salvation is all unto God and God alone. As a matter of fact, when you take out Christ you are an antichrist. You must remember what John said: that anyone who denies Christ is an anti-Christ.

Therefore, when you either deny Christ or say you have never sinned, you are an antichrist. We cannot do without Christ. He is the author of all. In Luther and Calvin, it is discovered that we sin because we are sinners. We are no good on our own. No good comes from us alone. All I am saying is that salvation is of God and God alone.

We cannot forget that it is because of God that we are saved. The sin is covered, but make no mistake; our hearts and minds can become wicked at the drop of a hat.

Galatians (2:10) says, "For whosoever shall keep the whole law, and yet offend in one point, he is guilty of all." This scripture says that we only need to do one thing wrong to be sinners. It is not the amount of sin that makes us sinners, it's just who we are.

On another point, there are those who say they need no grace just the law – such is Antinomianism. This states that because of Christ we need not follow any law, even the laws of the land. Such a frame of mind will only make you a rogue of the gospel. Cults and off-gospel churches have emerged throughout our day in this spirit.

Christ came to fulfill the law, not destroy it. In point, because he came to redeem the law, we ought not to kill another who does not follow the law according to our doctrine or interpretation. This is why it is so wrong how we crucify others for our own gain. We crucify for bigger churches. We put others down so that people will see us instead of Christ. It is dog eat dog in the house of God. No longer is God supreme—He has been replaced by our ambitions.

We kill and plunder, all for the glory of God. Beware, Crusaders. When we rebuke others we are wrong. When we put others down, we do the same to ourselves.

If we understand Luther, we will act in love and not in condemnation. When we act according to love, we bring to light Kant's categorical imperative. Which says in essence that we have a moral being within ourselves that guides us to do what is right.

Yet given to our own desires, we would not last. Given to our own way, we would not do right. We need God's grace upon our lives to help live well. We have lied to the world long enough that all is well in the camp of Christ. We have not only lied but also told each other there is nothing wrong with our behavior toward one another. We must turn things around, we must heed God.

We must let the world know that God is still working on His church. Did not the Bible proclaim that judgment must first begin in the house of God? I Peter 4:17 declares this. If we were as perfect as we declare, why would judgment need to be in the house of God FIRST?

The answer is because there is sin in the camp of God. It is one thing to have sin, but it is an abomination to not even recognize it and call it out.

Luke (18:13) says "And the publican, standing afar off, would not lift up so much as his eyes unto heaven, but smote upon his breast, saying, God be merciful to me a sinner." Maybe we skipped this Bible verse but this is the difference between church and sinner.

The Pharisees thought it was I and not God.

This is why it is so important to use the terms sinner and saint—it keeps us humble. We cannot take credit for anything. We just have to say thank you and give all credit to him. We cannot take this credit.

God hates pride; it reminds him of Lucifer. Yes, you walk in pride when you do not accept the theology of saint and sinner. In essence, you are calling your self just without God. There is no way we can go without his washing. We all need God to go from glory to glory.

In point, God is the only one that can call us just. We cannot call ourselves such, only God can save you, not yourself or the church. Since God gives justice, he also gives the peace of God.

We can try all we want and our actions would be futile. Men and women, through cults and teachings, have tried to connect to God in their own way without any great accomplishments. Again, their actions were futile. Nothing has changed today. Man cannot save himself.

The publican had five I's in his prayer. This shows how full this person was of himself. Too many Christians are full of themselves. They are spiritually overweight because they spend more time at the kitchen table than in the field.

This is why this is a powerful book—because it reminds us that we are sinful before the Lord. I cannot say I, I must say Him and Him alone.

1 John says (2:2) "And he is the propitiation for our sins: and not for ours only, but also for the sins of the whole world." Propitiation means satisfaction. In point, Christ alone satisfied sin. He became sin so that we could have liberty. No grace, no liberty.

Romans (3:25) says "Whom God hath set forth to be a propitiation through faith in his blood, to declare his righteousness for the remission of sins that are past, through the forbearance of God"

1 John (4:10) says "Herein is love, not that we loved God, but that he loved us, and sent his Son to be the propitiation for our sins."

Christ is the only atonement for sin. We have never been nor ever will be the atonement of ourselves. In fact, that is the very thing that got us in trouble (tree in the Garden). God used another tree 2000 years ago to bridge us back to him. The tree of good and evil was transformed to the tree of life once it was touched by blood. Not just any blood, either, but the blood of Jesus.

When we identify ourselves as sinner and saint, we tell God thank you. We cannot then beat up a sinner or saint who has fallen because we are all the same. The DNA is still in us. The DNA of Sin and Shame will never go away.

Isaiah (64:6) says "But we are all as an unclean thing, and all our righteousnesses are as filthy rags; and we all do fade as a leaf; and our iniquities, like the wind, have taken us away." This scripture, unknown to many, addresses when a woman is on her menstrual cycle.

The point I am trying to make is that a woman can be fine as wine but she has this monthly flow of blood. It is not a pretty sight to any, including the woman. Yet this filthy period can flow from a woman while she is dressed up in the sexiest outfit. She is flowing with blood but externally her husband may still desire her.

This is the message of Luther. We are pretty but our sins and our faults remind us of ourselves. For reasons unknown, we forgot about our fallen nature and our messed up lives. This is why I am trying to get people to see that we Christians are still on the toilet.

In fact, if you do not use the toilet or expel waste you will die quite soon from toxic death. All I am saying we are new creatures but we are creatures that still crap. When we were babies, we wore diapers but now that we are mature persons, we can go to the bathroom on our own.

Not passing waste will cause viral and bacterial issues

within our bodies. If you do not pass waste, you will die. Well, the same is true spiritually. When we do not confess and lay aside every sin and weight, we head toward a spiritual death.

This may explain why so many are falling away from the gospel—because they think once saved they have no further problems of sin. However, such is not the case. That is why I am writing this book. We all have vices. The worst thing you can do is to hide your vice. When you hide your vice, you only back up what needs to come out. This is especially true when you give a false impression of perfection to the world. No one has it all going on. We all deal with this mess called sin.

However, in the redemption of Christ, we can need with it. How can we deal with sin if we do not recognize that we still have this sinful nature? Historically, humanity has seen the results of untreated sewage. Diseases have come to the forefront of our lives because of non-professional waste management. What I am trying to say is that we as Christians need waste management. We have things within us that we do not like. And this flesh suit is a kicker that keeps on hitting us.

Yes, you can deny the flesh all you want but it still comes back the next day wanting more. In addition, I have found that those who say they have kicked the flesh habit are the most arrogant and self-righteous persons of all. It is wrong to deny sin. When you do so you are saying that you do not stink and everything that you do is great. This is not truthful in any way.

We all defecate. In the natural physical sense as well as in the spiritual. We all have things in our lives that we are constantly getting rid of. No one defecates **one time** in their life, neither does a Christian confess his sins only one time. It is an ongoing thing. If you never release your sin through confession, you will die because you are not being honest and not speaking the truth.

Which again is why the title of this book is so strong. I am trying to say we all still sin and make mistakes. We do not practice sin but we still sin in and through our lives.

Defecating is caused by eating. The more you eat the more you defecate. Do we need to eat the word of God? Do we not meditate on it day and night? If that is true, and it is, then we should be defecating or passing the waste from our lives daily.

Yet in 2008, there are many constipated Christians who swear they do not sin or do any wrong. They walk around as if they have never wiped themselves. This is not true. If the word of God is flowing through me from beginning to end, than I should be confessing and not walking around as if I am perfect and that I have no sin within me.

Many issues can come from not defecating, including faecal incontinence, obstructed defecation, and degenerative neuromuscular disorders. Well, many spiritual disorders can and will come about when you are not honest to yourself and God. A part of pride starts to grow in areas that will be hard to recover from.

We humans are depraved. We have no good bone in our bodies. We are wrong from the jump. No doubt that after salvation we must learn to confess not just to other believers but also to the world. We must let the world know that we are not perfect. We must let them see the scars and rags that God covers.

I remember a porn star saying that she had the word *__forgiven__* tattooed on her arm. This was to let her know that God forgives. Yes, he does, but God is also a God of justice and judgment. In addition, the Bible says that judgment must first begin in the house of God. It starts here. The toilet bowl of life does not begin in the streets it starts in the church.

When waste is not passed the fecal matter hardens within our bodies. This is what I believe God is trying to show us. We are becoming hard instead of soft. When God works on us, we should be getting better and not bitter. I have seen myself go through periods of bitterness and when I did, I became hard.

Yet for this love to go through, I must expel. I must let go of the waste, the wrong in my life, and see the power of God at work. This is why God needs to work on us and let the words of godly men come in and correct us to help expel the wrongs in our lives.

In other words, you and I should be able to repent and

confess when either God or man corrects. If you cannot take correction, you are immature and will not succeed. Many Christians are in that position with critical and damaged attitudes. This must change by the power of God. We must be saved by grace but mercy yet wipes us clean repeatedly.

The word rags means vesture. In other words I have priestly or costly robes on but I am a sinner yet even when enlightened by the spirit. I am saint and yet a sinner.

Our best is not good enough. We think our merits can do something for us, however; in the scheme of things, they do not mean anything at all. We cannot escape the point that the only thing that we have is repentance. I look over my life and see nothing good. The word of God says that there is none that is righteous or holy. The only righteous person is God himself.

Salvation shows us how messed up we are, not how good we are. It shows us how the power of God is needed upon our lives. God gave us something that we did not deserve and could not do on our own. Therefore, because I deserve death and hell, it should make me want to be in love with God and press people toward the power of His love. This is why all who negate the gospel deserve Hell as the finally point of God's Judgment.

We are tainted and smell because of sin. Sin is present in our camps and because of our nature, we have to deal with it, yet through imputation, we have life with Christ.

We no longer have to go around with low heads. I can lift my head and shout, redeemed! However, if I shout redeemed, I must say from what and by whom. This is the evangelism that I need to demonstrate. Yes, I have been redeemed because of my sins and wrongs.

Psalms 49:7, 15 speaks to the matter that I cannot redeem myself; only God can. I cannot take a God problem and get a man-made solution. Since Christ thought his blood was the answer and solution, how dare I walk around as if I got it all?

In fact, I have nothing. Only God redeems me from sin. Because He redeems me, I cannot act as if all is done by me. No sir or madam, I did not redeem myself.

Zechariah (3:1) says "And he showed me Joshua the high priest standing before the angel of the LORD, and Satan standing at his right hand to resist him.(3:2) And the LORD said unto Satan, The LORD rebuke thee, O Satan; even the LORD that hath chosen Jerusalem rebuke thee: is not this a brand plucked out of the fire? (3:3) Now Joshua was clothed with filthy garments and stood before the angel" this scripture to me is the essence of Luther's message to humankind. The message of saint and sinner.

Not only is the high priest standing with filthy gags, Satan is not on the left but the right side, which represents the side of power. He is abusing the high priest yet God rebukes Satan even before we know that he is filthy.

In the Old Testament, the high priest had to be clean.

When unclean, a high priest could not serve. Yet here is God rebuking Satan even though the high priest has broken God's law. How powerful that looks. Satan in reality was right to want to get rid of us because he knew our potential. What makes this decision powerful is that it was made under divine counsel. In other words, God made this decision to call us blessed when we were dirty. I like to assume that this was not Joshua's first time coming into God's presence.

Verse 4 shows us that Joshua on his own could not get rid of his sin. As Joshua could not, so we cannot. If the Jewish high priest could not be clean, how can we?

This tells us that we as Christians need a redeemer and his name is Jesus. The high priest was messed up but he yet belonged to God as we do today.

One commentary points out the Joshua has no priestly things on; just a turban. This suggests it had never been about spiritual clothes, but is about the person himself. Priestly clothes cannot cover sins. My clothes or titles are not enough to cover my sins, only God has the right and power to wash away my sins.

Since God is the suffering servant, how dare I walk around as if I have no sin? Yes, I am sinful but this is why Christ is on the right hand side of God making intercessions—because the accuser (Satan) is after us.

The application is plain. We must stop pointing to the world and pointing out the sins of others without them letting them see our sins first.

We must let them now that as good as they think Christians are, we need a savior. We need a lawyer to whom to speak and cover our sin. When we can show forth, we can show our place and show that God is working on us. We must tell the world we still use the bathroom and that because of Christ alone, we are free.

Ezekiel 16:49

King James Version "Behold, this was the iniquity of thy sister Sodom, pride, fullness of bread, and abundance of idleness was in her and in her daughters, neither did she strengthen the hand of the poor and needy. And they were haughty, and committed abomination before me: therefore I took them away as I saw well."

For all my years of being in ministry, I thought the reason why God destroyed Sodom was homosexuality. But according to Ezekiel, this was not the case. Homosexuality was not the initial sin that got God's attention. What got God's attention was pride, fullness of bread, and idleness.

For all my years, I was looking at the effect and not the cause of the sin. As Christians, we are like Eli; very quick to judge people quickly before we get to know why they are going through the pain in their lives.

Eli was corpulent. Maybe he was more concerned about his belly than those who were in need. We need to change things and not worry about our bellies but about others around us. The church for too long has justified overeating and has ignored the sins of envy and strife.

This is why this book is written—to help Christians see things from another side, and that side includes looking at ourselves first and then at other people. To be honest, if we examined ourselves more we would have less time to judge others.

Yet again, we all must fight the spirit of Eli, the spirit of judgment. Hannah had to fight the Eli spirit, but others have not had the strength of Hannah and because of the word of Eli, they have left the church. We forgot that we used the same toilet that everyone else used.

In my thinking, Eli was a curmudgeon. He was full of stubborn ideas to the point that his first judgment was wrong about Hannah. In truth, how many times have we judged a brother wrongly? How many times have we torn down instead of lifting up? If we cannot lift up the body of Christ, how can we lift up the world of sinners? We cannot do it alone.

How powerful it is that we judge people for going to the same bathroom that we are not finished using. The main idea of this book is to let Christians know that we are not better but for the grace of God there go I. This should be our prayer, this should be our sight into a dying nation.

Remember Matthews 20 of that Pharisees and publican who were in the house of God, and the Pharisees bragged while the publican asked for forgiveness. This is the state of the church today.

We have more people bragging about how many saved there are than people reaching for souls and teaching them amazing grace and not self-grace. We are not saved by our own actions; we are all saved by the grace of God.

There but for the Grace of God go I, should be our idiom for life. We cannot count others out because we are here by His grace. We only move and speak by His grace but because we are so easily tempted to judge, we do not see others beyond ourselves.

However, back to the main scripture; homosexuality was the end but pride was the beginning of the sin. The four vices of pride, excess, idleness, and abomination were the cause of homosexuality.

My God, we in America are full of pride and overabundance. We have mega church, mega cars, and mega divorces; more than we can handle and we still cry out for more. Well, according to scripture, this brings on abomination.

In America, we have preachers preaching about abominations but we have not gotten to the core of the abomination. We must start at the four vices of men and women.

Perhaps if we can reexamine how we look at things, we can find a key to the issues that we see today. Again, the scripture pointed to the four vices. We have to re-think things, my brother and sister. We have to change things around and speak loudly that we must rebuke pride. The church has too long gone after the symptoms and not the cause of sin in the lives of people.

Sodomites, because of their riches, had it at ease. They were so caught up with their things that they followed abomination. What does this say to the church? It says that we must not be at ease from our own stuff and forget to continue to seek the Lord.

We can never say we have arrived. We cannot be like the man who built his barn (Luke 12:16-20) and said that I am going to rest and chill. God said to him "you fool, this night your soul will be required of thee." Well this is what God is saying to us—that we must change our ways and stop having confidence in our money, popularity, and such. We must continue to seek the Lord.

Did not the Bible say to seek ye first the kingdom of heaven? Did not the Bible say for us to not covet our neighbor's wife? That is exactly what we have done. We want more than what God has given to us. We cannot be content with the things that we have. For too long we have this desire for more things and yet this is what caused Sodom to turn to homosexuality.

Again, this is a powerful revelation that says we must look at ourselves again and see God working things out in our lives. However, because we have been full of ourselves, we have not seen that what we have corrupts us over time.

The brass snake that saves can turn around and be the

same snake that kills. American preachers, hear me. It was not homosexuality by itself. It was pride and the three vices that lead to the sin of homosexuality. Homosexuality is still a sin, but we cannot only hit homosexuality and forget about the root causes of this sin.

This again is why this book is so important. It is going to tell Christians to stop going after the big fish and just learn to humble themselves before the Lord. I have often wondered why anointed people can be so prideful that when the power of God comes they do not bow or acknowledge His presence. They show no more honor or glory to His name. We have to change the corner my brothers and sisters, and really look at ourselves.

The four vices are so strong that they do not look at the needs of others. In point, they become self and do not look unto God. This is why the sin of homosexuality came upon the nation of Sodom—because the seed was planted in the ground of pride.

They become so engulfed in themselves that they could not see the needs of others around them. Is this not our churches sometimes? We see our program and our needs and we never see the needs of the nation. I believe the time has come to have a change of heart.

Selfishness goes along with pride. They work the same together in life. If you are in pride, you are going to have selfishness, and not too far away is homosexuality. If every man and woman knew that if they continued in their sinning homosexuality would come down the road, people would stop the four vices in their life. If we said that we do not want homosexuality then we would say no to the four vices that bring forth the sin of homosexuality.

Verse 50 said that they also become puffed up with pride or haughtiness. They become puffed up with their own property. What do we see in our churches? We see al-lot of pride. We see a lot of 'look of what we have in life': Look at my car, my congregation; I am one church in 25,000 locations. No, we must keep God as the center of our lives. Glory is not unto us but unto God and God alone.

Gluttony is one of the four vices that brought forth homosexuality. Overeating is still a sin. The sodomites ate, drank, and did other things in excess. This scripture tells us that excess will kill us. They were at ease in Sodom. Sodom was relaxing and they enjoyed their greatness. We must look at our things and say, look at what we have and it came from God alone.

As one Mathew Henry commentary said, the idleness was like still waters that gather filth. This is what happened in Sodom and what happened in Sodom is happening to us as well. Our waters have been so stilled that we have gathered all types of filth and problems.

We must change our attitudes and mind frames. We must change our way of thinking. We must not just go to the toilet but we must wipe and be clean. We cannot just look at others, we must look ourselves.

I truly believe we in the body of Christ have a spiritual dementia. We have no idea what is flesh and what is God when it comes to telling the truth and treating our neighbor right. Everything is justified.

Nothing is sinful anymore. I admit with all that is within me that I am full of sin and not perfect yet there are those who walk around as if they have never sinned in their lives. They walk on water and expect others to follow.

Dementia is caused by a loss of brain cells and normal things cannot be done anymore. Things that should be done easily and regularly are done only with much work. Dementia is impairment. I believe the body of Christ has come to these points.

We know how to shout and study but we hate another brother. Not only do we hate, we plan his or her fall. We get on the phone and gossip. We are ready to kill at the drop of a hat. We do all these things and, most importantly, feel no guilt in the process.

Where is the soul? Where is compassion? We see our brother fall one time and we are ready to impeach him or her. Yet God has forgiven us 7 times 70 but we refuse to give that same forgiveness to one another.

We give correction but even when the brother or sister changes, we treat them differently. Yes, this is dementia and it is throughout our churches. We want all to hold us up and pray for us, but we do not want to help another person. God help us; God help us.

We do not need another praise service we need a service about forgiveness and loving where we confess our sins one to another. We have made praise the major order of the day. No, it should be Christ and loving one another. That is the only order of the day.

Another thing about dementia is that it is related to getting older. I truly believe that the older we get, the more we must fight this problem. It seems like when Christians get older they become more judgmental and unforgiving. They would rather see judgment than repentance. They would rather see the blood of a Christian than the blood of Christ. Where are we going with this type of thinking? We are going to be no longer the church but merely a club.

In addition, because of the actions of some, young Christians are getting a raw deal on what it is to be saved. God help us. We would rather kill than pray. We would rather hate than love. What is wrong with the body of Christ? I tell you, it's spiritual dementia. We must deal with such actions to stop this. This is why we are in the bathroom—because we have not fully learned how to love one another. If you have learned, then let the world know about receiving and giving forgiveness.

Dementia also includes memory loss. There are many Christians who have lost the memory of God's love toward them. Not only have they forgotten the forgiveness of God of their souls, but also they believe they are always right and have no forgiveness toward others. In addition, they think everybody around them is wrong. They cannot speak or spell "I am sorry". Sorry is not in their vocabulary. Repenting to another brother is totally out of the question. We have to change these values.

This is a vein to the issue that Christians are going to the bathroom. In God's presence they love and show compassion. However, in man's presence they demonstrate hate and bitterness. When will this madness stop? When will we learn that the gate is narrow? In addition, that narrow gate is built on love. If we do not love or forgive our brother, we will not make it into heaven. No matter how gifted or smart we may be.

Dementia is a slow process and what has been done is going away slowly. For the record, I would like to let you know that every now and then I suffer from dementia. If we are honest, all of us suffer from this problem every now and then in our lives.

We get into our titles, pulpit, and possessions, and we forget about the way God has dwelt with us. Instead of loving God we come down hard on others Yes, we are found lacking.

I take this pause because I do not want anyone to think I have arrived or have reached ascension. In the corner, I take a page from Paul and say that I am chief of sinners. I write this book not to condemn per se, but to get us to talk and stir into action for change in our lives. I do not want a revival. I am looking for a reformation.

Revivals only affect churches, but reformations affect the entire city. This is what I desire and want of the Lord. So again, I write not as one who has arrived but as one who is trying to get there from the first and second command.

According to answers.com, dementia is not a disease but a syndrome. In other words, dementia is a group of symptoms. So in fact, dementia is just the result of something. Well, can we be honest? Spiritual dementia comes from the lack of love in the body of Christ.

We have buildings and possessions. We have robes and popularity. But these things have killed off our love and commitment to one another and to Christ. We have to answer to Christ for this problem.

When we see ourselves in bitterness, gossip, and killing one another, we are on the road to spiritual dementia. And if we continue, we will only be shells of ourselves when life is done. One way to keep dementia at bay is to stay active when we become lazy and idle. We cannot forget, it was idleness that got David into trouble.

In point, this scripture warns us about being full. We must be full of the spirit and not the things of life. We must check our guts and say we are not here for people but for the glory and honor of God.

The amplified Bible talks about how she has prosperous ease. In other words, once you gain, it becomes an important point of your objectivity. But the only object should be Christ. We are told that we are stewards. What we have does not belong to us but to Him. This is why it is so important that we are not caught in our full. When we are caught in our full we become slow and nonchalant about things.

As I mentioned before, David got in trouble because he was chilling out when the rest of his men were at war. They were doing and he was not doing. They were unsatisfied with what they had while David was satisfied. We must be careful that our ultimate satisfaction comes from the Lord and Him alone.

We cannot be at ease. If anything, we must be like bloodhounds as we seek the Lord. Bloodhounds do not stop but continue to go on and on and on. We cannot let anything stop us from seeking His passion and will.

Too many Christians are looking out the window rather than at the mirror. It is so easy to look upon others and judge them, yet the best example we can give is to show others change within and through ourselves. Did not Paul say that we are a living epistle? In other words, people read us. We need to look at the mirror and see our faults, wrinkles and problems within our lives and face them. When I say face them, I do not say it with arrogance but with a humble spirit as unto the Lord.

In a manner of speaking, we want spiritual **plastic surgery**. We want to cover up who we really are and in the meantime, here come baby Christians who do not know the amount of plastic surgery we have had to hide and cover the issues within our lives. I pray we melt away this mind frame.

People want to see the grace of God in action. Yet we Christians come across as though we need no grace. When the sinner sees this, they say there is no way they could come up to par with it.

People of God do use the bathroom. We need to tell Christians this point everywhere we go. We do sit on the toilet we do not hover. We sit like every body else. We are not perfect. We need to throw away the plastic surgery in our life. We need to cry aloud and tell the world not to look to us but to Jesus the Christ who has imputed his love toward me.

While we were yet in our sins, Christ died for us. This is something that is strong and true within and throughout my life. The Lord gave me a chance and I need to be a walking testimony to this fact. We can so wrapped up in our stuff that we can fall pray to our own devices in life.

Again, this gives the picture of water that is stagnate and going nowhere. We must prepare ourselves to go somewhere in the Lord. We must not have a haughty spirit but a sharing spirit. If God shared with us, we must also share with others. If God gave to us, we must also give to others. We cannot do anything different. We must share the blessing of the Lord.

In point, we must become the antithesis of hypocrites who brag about how saved they are. We must do more than only pointing out how well we adhere to the gospel. In this way we will counter those who say "Look how perfect I am". We say in essence "Do not look at me but look at Christ the author and finisher of our faith".

This sharing goes two ways. We must not allow the devil to put a stopgap into our hands or pockets. The devil must not distract us with worldly things. We must always give forth the power of God in and through our lives so that souls as a whole will be saved and delivered. Yet this happens one day at a time by giving back and sharing the blessing of God.

We must remember that we use the toilet too. We cannot just keep the toilet to ourselves, confess our sins, know God has heard them, then turn around to one another and tell them that God has not heard them.

The devil is a liar. The same God that loves me is the same God that loves everybody else. We must not be so caught up in ourselves that we do not see our brothers in need.

As I need the toilet so does my fellow man. It seems like Christians are taking on the attitude "I got it so you get it for yourself". I never forget the quote "I got mine so it's time for them to get their own stuff".

That type of mind fame cannot help, it can only hurt. We must say in essence that we are all human. None is better than another. The calling upon my life is by God's grace and I must not walk around like a peacock, I must tell people that Jesus can save them too.

John 8

This story, even though only mentioned in the gospel of John, shows more than anything the central theme of my book. Here you have a woman who is caught dead wrong but you see the master run to her rescue. Where there should have been judgment, grace and mercy was given.

In point, Jesus knew the hearts of these Pharisees and Sadducees. During his whole ministry, they never acknowledged him as high priest, but in their self-loathing act, they came to him looking for judgment.

Christ saw beyond their sins. As Christ did, so should we. How dare we become so engrossed with God that we fail to see the grace he has given to us? How can we forget that we are here by His love and grace? We cannot afford to be absent minded. We must seek the savior and after we find Him, tell people of Him. This is why Christians use the bathroom too. We cannot be found unless we were lost. We cannot be saved unless we were condemned.

Yet with our grand scheme of thinking and acting, we

have lost sight of the love and power of Christ. The same love that Jesus gave us, we must extend toward others. We must tell a dying generation that we are not perfect. There are sins and issues within our lives that beset us on a daily basis. But by His grace, we are here today.

In *verse 1*, we see Christ set up camp at the Mount of Olives. This is the place of anointing. This is the place where kings are anointed to reign. Here in this most sacred place Jesus allowed sinners to come into his mountain. That is, they had to come up from the valley. We cannot forget that we all are coming up to Christ. No one is above Him.

We all have to press to him and not to ourselves. We cannot tell the world that only we can do this. Jesus said in John 15 "without me you could not do anything". So due to this we must preach that not only did He save us but He can save others as well. Yes, Christians have stains on them that only Christ can wash away. In Him, we have an advocate.

What gets me is that at the end of Chapter 7, every man went to his house but Jesus went to the mountain. This is the point. If we are not careful, we Christians will go to our comfort zone while Christ is going up higher.

I believe He calls us ever higher so that we can see how messed up we are and how depraved we are in our sins. As Isaiah saw the Lord so should we. In point, the closer we get to Christ, the more we should cry out that we are unholy.

Yet more often we cry out "look at me" instead of looking at the savior. My brothers and my sisters, it is not our face on the cross but that of Christ. This is why we cannot afford the infighting and small sins. These things divert our attention from Christ onto ourselves. We are not the stars; we are only His vessel to serve His purpose.

The mount of olive was a major hub for Christ. He rested there and prayed for God's will to be done. Yet, he allowed the judgment of a woman to take place in His place of peace. What should have been His down time instead He spent helping a woman to live again.

Dear friends, why do we give such a different picture of Christ? He came to save that which was lost. We must show the mercy of God to others rather than judge them. We must make this change for the world to see.

According to the New Unger Bible Handbook, John 8 was omitted in many manuscripts because the grace that Jesus showed this woman was unpalatable to later legalists. Many do not believe this passage took place because the grace in it is unbelievable. Yet as Christians, we should believe it because He does the same for us. My friends, we have to tell the body of Christ that yes, He did it for us. If we are going to be true Christians who go to the bathroom, we must yell to the world that yes, God saved us.

What amazes me about Christ is that he has this feeling about me after I was saved even though I have blown it more times than I can remember within my own life. We cannot but only give God thanks for this grace. Yet we become legalistic when we forget the continuing work that God does on us. We must stress the word continued—His grace has never stopped and never will stop. We must learn to see just our brother and not his sins under grace. We cannot see others' sins without seeing our own. God help us stop this nonsense of picking on each other's crap and forgetting that the King of Kings picks up ours at the same time.

I will be blunt and say that we Christians go to bathroom more than the sinner does. Why? The sinner is not in a cleaning motion, so he is constipated, yet we who are Christians continue to be cleaned by the word according to John 15. This cleaning, as we know, is not outside but inside. Physically, when we are cleaned, we pass more waste. This is what I am trying to alert us to; that we are full of crap and God's grace is continuing to clean us out.

Therefore, we have more crap to clean up because the more we see our savior we cry out undone. So if God can clean up after us, why can not we learn and do the same for our fellow man.

In *Verse 2*, we see the stage being set that Jesus does his judging at the temple. This brings such power to the text because it is the temple where religious activities took place. At this epicenter, something was going to be done as it related to Moses' law. Jesus could have waited to do this outside, but He wanted the showdown to happen within the temple.

We who are Christians need to show our shame not just

in our homes but also in the church. The temple was every-thing for the Jewish culture. We for some reason want to wear a mask that says we do not go to the bathroom in front of the church but if we should confess our sins anywhere, it should be in the house of God.

It is a problem when we walk in lies in the house of God. As the tabernacle and temple were a place for confession and being forgiven, we in 2008 if not careful will turn the temple and church into a fashion show. How saved am I? How powerful am I? There is no more humbleness, we brag of our great feats and accomplishments. These mind frames need to be rebuked. We are only fooling ourselves.

I suggest that maybe we take some time to clean and correct during our worship service. How can we truly wor-ship if our hands our dirty? We must keep our confession going even after salvation. God is in the temple. He is there to not only judge but also to give grace.

As we will see, Christ did not just judge but gave grace. This again is how Christians use the bathroom—we so want to point fingers without also pointing people to the foot of the cross. This may explain why our culture is so mad at us: we only give them a dose of judgment and not a dose of grace.

I suggest we give a dose of grace with judgment. The two go hand and hand. In this passage Jesus did not ignore the sin. We cannot ignore the sins in our lives but we must also see his grace for those who desire such. We cannot departmentalize these things. It all works together. The world is looking for a change and I believe we have the answer, but we must give them the whole answer.

And that answer must be demonstrated in how we deal with each other. How can we save the world if we are fighting and hurting one another for our own glory? We cannot keep this up. We cannot reach the world and kill our friends. Christ said they would know we are Christians by our love.

The word temple is hee-er-on in Greek, which means a sacred place. This was the sacred place from which Jesus wanted to show the world that even Christians use the bathroom. This was the showdown that God wanted to see and show His glory.

Miracles are not just healing the sick; the foremost miracle is the forgiveness of sin. The greatest miracle is how we deal with one another to keep the unity of the saints. Yet it is because we are trying to hide our sins that we are not able to help others who so need to hear and believe our gospel. At the temple court, a judgment was going to be put in place with the power of imputation.

In *verse 3*, we see the Scribes and Pharisees bring a woman to Jesus. The scribes were there to record the event and give reading to the Mosaic Law. Yet Jesus saw the double team and won the battle. He saw what they were up too. In point, the church folk wanted the woman to die.

What type of culture do we have in our churches that we now want people to fail? We do not want them to find grace, we want them to end up on the cutting block. How far have we fallen in that we are now looking for executions instead of redemption? In point, they came to Christ as an angry mob looking for blood. We should look for blood but it should be the blood of Christ and not of the sinner or brother.

Yes, they brought the sinner to Jesus but their evangelism was messed up. Our evangelism is to bring to Christ and not to destroy them. Again, this is why we must understand that we are yet sinners saved by grace. According to the NIV Study Bible, they could have kept the woman hidden while they talked to Jesus but no, they wanted to embarrass her in front of Jesus and others.

This again points to why Christians should be full of grace and not judgment. If God had exposed our sins we would not be in our current situation. We could not hold up our heads for anything because God would have exposed us. In my walk with God, I have noticed that those who that want to expose a particular sin have committed that sin themselves. This is why Christ said for us to judge ourselves before we jump on somebody else. If we really looked at ourselves, we would do things differently to other people.

Instead of crucifying ourselves, we want to crucify others. This is not the will of God. The will of God is to move away from this crucifying. Yes, we have the wood and nails but they are for ourselves and not for others. The nails and cross are for me and my own sins. Jesus said "take up your cross and follow me".

Just a side point; this passage of taking up your cross is in Matthew 16:24, Mark 8:34, Mark 10:21, and Luke 9:23. The cross to carry was the horizontal cross. This means a lot to me because the horizontal represents how we deal with one another. When we are walking with the cross, we have less time to point to the sins of others.

Jesus did not say this to warm his vocal cords; he knew how preoccupied we would get in our own works and goals. In addition, the cross keeps us humble and not haughty. Yet repeatedly, we see our friends; sins and not our own.

This is why we need the cross displayed before and under the altar. If people saw our crosses on our backs, instead of a cross on chain around our necks, things would be different in Christianity. We would have less time to talk and more time to pray for not only ourselves but also people in our lives.

If you carry a cross, you can bet that there will be a crucifixion. The two things go together. There is no separation of the two. Yet we have men and women in our church who are carrying a cross without crucifixion.

In addition, when you walk with a cross people will make fun of you along the way. Nevertheless, is it imperative to let people know that we Christians are not perfect. History has been full of men who have tried to beat the drum of perfection and have not lasted the first quarter of life. The reason we bear our cross is to remind ourselves that God is still working on us. Again, we need to take up the cross and follow Christ.

Because we do not have a cross on our backs, we are more preoccupied with others who sin. If we had our cross and carried it, we would not feel so much like spending our energy on beating up other Christians and sinners.

In *Verse 4*, He sees the woman caught in the very act. In other words, there was no feeling that it did not happen. She was guilty, but so was the man. As in the past, men have always picked one person and left out the other. This is powerful because all have sinned. We can look at the **world** and call it a sin but when **Christians** do it, we call it a mistake or fault. Sorry sir, sin is sin. There is no redefining the wrong.

However, in Christianity we categorize our sins as good and bad or little or great. Sin is sin. All sin is punishable by death. We cannot change the rules in mid stream. Yes, Christians do sin. Yes, Christians perform abominations that are not pleasing in God's eyes. Yes, Christians use the bathroom. If anything, we should look at the grace of God upon our lives and say aloud if God forgave us, He can and will forgive others.

Deuteronomy 22:22 was given by Moses to speak of stoning both women and men who committed the sin of adultery. Already the Pharisees were wrong because they only brought the woman to Jesus for judgment.

This is a great example of people interpreting His word to make themselves feel good while others are left in the cold. You cannot pass out different judgment. This is an unbalanced scale, no question.

God hates an unbalanced scale. Yet every day we see Christian politics. A preacher dies and his unsaved son or daughter gets the position of pastor. A bishop dies and an unqualified relative gets the position. A man or woman pays a certain amount of money and gets the position. Such work is a sign of an unbalanced scale. God cannot tolerate such.

Come, Christians, follow me to the bars, adult book stores, and other places of iniquity to tell men and women that Jesus saves. In addition, we all struggle in sin but God forgives. We must tell men and women to lay aside every weight and sin that so easily puts us down. Yes, Christians have sins and weights but God's grace is powerful.

In *verse 5*, we see the legalism of the teachers. There was no grace, just judgment. They quoted Moses and said it was a done deal. What Jesus said was that if this was so why did they not kill her and him at the place the act? He pointed out that there was no need to do it at the temple. He said that they should not desecrate the temple area with such sins. Jesus knew their hearts. He knew they wanted to elevate themselves by showing the sins of another.

In today's world, this has not changed: we are more interested in finding sin instead of showing people the better way. We would rather point out the sins of others and not see our own. This must change. We cannot continue in this way. This again is why this book handles the "forgotten" sins of men.

In reading the scripture verses you hopefully will see things in a new light. You will hopefully see how we all need His grace and mercy in and through out lives. Again, in looking at the law, the stoning was only for a betrothed virgin (Deuteronomy 22:23 – 24). I think we can deduct that this was no virgin that they were about to stone.

How powerful that Jesus was born of a virgin! Perhaps Jesus wondered if Mary and Joseph had stayed they might have stoned his mother and ended grace.

What a powerful revelation to share that Jesus might have seen his mother in this woman. The point is if the angel had not come down and spoke with Joseph, Mary would have been stoned. We Christians judge too early. We do not let work have its perfect work. Rather we jump to conclusions. This is not the will of God. For when we prejudge we may miss a miracle that is about to take place.

Philippians 1 and 6 says to be confident that God is able to complete what He has performed. There is no doubt in my mind that God can and will do this. I think we expect people to jump up like spring Christians over night.

If God worked with our foolishness, then what is wrong with us today?. We are Christians who use the bathroom but it's Christ who flushes the sin.

According to Dake, this was the 67th question in the New Testament. The question to Jesus was answered in His blood and not that of our own. It was answered because He saved us. It was answered on Calvary.

We should point people and their sins to Calvary. Yes, the church is a good start but the result is Christ and Him alone. He is the only advocate to take away the sins of the world. No Christ means no tomorrow. With Christ, there is a tomorrow.

In *verse 6*, we see the only record of Jesus' writing. In addition, he does this not for a believer but a sinner that needs forgiveness. How powerful that is that Christ wrote for a sinner. This is why we Christians use the bathroom.

If Christ showed compassion to her, why is it hard for us to show compassion to others? We have to stop this attitude of being holier than others. We all need Christ to stop the lynch mob. If Christ had said one thing, they would have attacked and killed that woman but he slowed their roll instead.

We need to slow our roll before people attack and hurt us. We need to move from where we are to where we need to go in and through our lives. As Christ had patience with that woman, we need to have patience with other people. We should look at people and consider ourselves. We are not better but only saved and blessed by His grace. This is how we can turn the corner of reaching souls for the kingdom of God.

Too many Christians have an Andreas Bodenstein (Karlstadt) mentality. Karlstadt was a friend of Luther during the Reformation but turned into a zealot in destroying the paintings of the time. Luther had to correct the brother and put him on the right track. In 1522, this transaction took place yet today there are people who are so zealous that they do not have the time and patience for others as they walk with God. Many forget about the love and power that God showed to them. They want to destroy anything that looks evil. This is good but must be done with wisdom.

From the NIV Study Bible Notes, it is said that the finger of God wrote the laws in Exodus 31. So did Jesus write the laws down. No one knows what he wrote but it must have lined up with mercy, grace, and justification because in the end that was what happened to the adulterous woman.

As in the scarlet letter, people wanted to put the Scarlet A on that woman, but Christ, instead of branding the woman, branded the crowd. Is it possible we are so into ourselves that we do not see the love of God that needs to be expanded abroad?

In *verse 7*, we see the main text. Where are the words that ring throughout time? It says if you have no guilt, you can throw the stones. Yet if you have guilt or sin, you are rebuked. Some have even speculated that the man who committed the adultery was one of the church leaders. No one knows who he was. The only thing certain is before you point the finger at someone else first point at yourself.

Learn to turn the Bible on yourself and not on others first. We are to lead by example.

When the crowd approached, Jesus was sitting and writing but when we was ready to speak he arose. Right there that should have told the convicts to watch out because the Old Testament said let God arise and let his enemies be afraid.

Well this is what is about to happen to us. Jesus is about to stand up. My Christian friends, if Christ was able to stand for you, why block Christ for standing for others? When we act self-righteous, we stand for ourselves instead of Christ and so people see us instead of Christ. Yet when we admit our faults and tell the world we are saved by grace, all things must conclude in a better way.

This is what drives this book. Let people see your scars and flesh wounds and show them what the Lord has done in and around their lives. For whatever you are or going to do, let it be marvelous in and through our eyes. We want people to see Jesus. As the Greeks told Philip of their desire to see Jesus, we must demonstrate such a life that they want Jesus and not us. We are only the moon, he is the Son.

They continued to question, which says if they had stopped maybe Christ would have said nothing. But they could not leave well enough alone. They kept shouting for judgment and Christ stood for righteousness. We must do the same thing. We must stand for him always. Yet the church has turned into the chorus of killing instead of the chorus of mercy and grace. We must turn our attention from such things.

When are we going to stop? Do we identify sin, the answer is yes, but to beat up another person in the body is not well accomplished. Remember the scripture that the strong should bear the infirmities of the weak. It is easier to throw stones than to bind the broken wounds of a person. It seems we have come to an age in which we would rather kill than heal. We would rather destroy than help. We would rather correct than lead.

What happened to Isaiah on the day when he said woe is me because I am undone? Too many Christians are crying out that they are done. They are crying out as if they have arrived. They not only claim that they have arrived but they also yell aloud that they got it too. No one has it but Christ.

He is the only sinless creature that every lived. Again, I am not saying to not label sin. I am saying when you do label, do it in the same manner that God does it to you. It's like sharks in the water that wait for blood. If we would look on that sinner as ourselves, there would be less violence in the world. We all must come to the realization that we are all eternally flawed.

Yes, we have Christ but we also have a dead nature that lives and breathes inside of us. We must put down our stones and take up our crosses. Have we forgotten Hebrews 3:13? John Piper got me hipped to this. This passage says to exhort one another every day.

We all must examine ourselves in this point. Are we killing one another every day? Are we praying for one another every day? Alternatively, do we gossip every day?

The word of God said to exhort one another. We have strayed a long way from this passage. Oh, God help us to understand that our ministry is always behind closed doors. This is why we are Christians who are still messing up because at times we kill instead of exhorting. We tear down instead of exhorting. We have to be honest. When we do not exhort, we are on the toilet. We are in the bathroom.

Let us be honest, if more people are leaving the churches versus coming to it, the answer is not because of Christ. The answer is due to either Pastor or members or both. Since the failure is not with God, we must seek the Lord for to resolve these issues in our own lives.

God is not into the shaming of people, He is into the redemption of humankind. How can we point out other people's sins without seeking and smelling our own? It cannot be done.

Even Christians use the bathroom says we all have shame. All will tell you that there is some level of shame when you go to the bathroom. You do not want all to know your business. In fact, most try to hide when they go to the bathroom. Yet such mind frames cause problems down the road. As Christ has covered us so ought we to cover each other. Again, if Christ covers us why should we not cover the other person? We do not want to participate because we want to be the only person standing. We want all the glory ourselves.

In *Verse 8*, we see Jesus again writing things down. This is the second time he writes his words into the sand. We can only speculate what he wrote but maybe the first time he wrote he wrote thou shalt love thy God and the second time he wrote love thy neighbor as thy self.

This brings up again the key concept of this book, which is that every Christian should love one another without pointing the finger at the other person. In reality, you cannot continue to point the finger and not hit yourself at the same time.

Jesus also went down on his knees because he was getting ready for them to walk away. He knew that they were about to leave the scene because he had touched a nerve. Maybe an issue in the church is that we are touching nerves and we are not saying ouch. As Christians, we cannot walk around as if all is well and not spell out the pain that is within our lives. We must first believe that we are guilty and not only ask forgiveness but also try to heal this pain center in our lives.

In point, when God touches a nerve do not walk around as if all is well. Let the people see the scars. When we walk around as if we have none it gives perspective to the world that we are perfect and that is far from the truth. God is working on us every day and thank God He is.

In *verse 9*, we must allow the spirit of God to convict people. For too long we have done this ourselves and have caused more problems. The word of God said that their own conscience got to them and hit them where it hurts. Sometimes we try too hard to get people to see their mistakes when in reality only the Holy Ghost can do this.

In the end, Jesus was standing alone. For too long, we are standing instead of just giving this person over to God and letting God deal with it. As God worked on us in private, we must allow others to do the same thing. We must let the spirit of God follow from head to toe. We must say Lord I preached it now you finish the work.

When we force change on someone instead of being convicted you are really not helping the person at all. In addition, when we look at people we do not need to use many words—just simple words to reach them for the work of the Lord. We cannot continue to hit them upside the head and expect them to get it.

When you continue to hit a baby without abandon that child will become brain dead. Therefore, we should not do the same thing in our lifetime. We must be careful and not try to take the place of the Holy Ghost. Only the spirit of God can draw and convict. We are not a part of the Trinity. You cannot force God on people; they must see their own sins.

Upon hearing the words of Christ, they started leaving from the oldest to the youngest. They left because they saw their own ugly sins.

In *verse 10*, all of her accusers are gone. They are gone because they see their own sins. How powerful that would be in the body of Christ if we all saw our sins first. How powerful it would be if we loved others, the way God loves us.

One issue that husbands deal with is putting the toilet head down and aiming right. When they do not they will have hell to pay for. We must say to all, we need to have the same thing toward a sinner or a fallen brother or sister.

You cannot continue to not be attentive toward the needs of another if you continue to be only concerned about yourself. You must overcome this issue and see God in this power and light. When you see people as you see yourself, you really get an understanding that we are all saved by his marvelous grace.

What is powerful is that this woman did sin. This is not made up but the master says to her "hath no man condemned thee". She was guilty, but because of Christ, she was not condemned.

As R.C. Sproul says, God has granted us foreign righteousness. We have not seen these things before. We have not experienced such types of grace in our lifetime. This is what God desires we give others. I am not talking about a nice handshake but the Lord really wants us to show forth His power by love and forgiveness. This woman is condemned but the Lord does not see the sin He sees the woman.

How can we translate such truths into our lives? We must see the person more than the sin. Yes, she is guilty. Yes, you and I are guilty. Yes, he is guilty but in Christ I see you more than I see the sin.

Saints of the highest God, why cannot we do the same thing? We know how to throw mud but we cannot throw a towel to wipe away the mud. We are Christians who use the bathroom. Every one of us have destroyed the bathrooms in our churches by our thoughts and actions, but God gives us grace.

If he does thus for us, what is our concern? We must move beyond pointing, and go forward in the love and power of the Lord Jesus Christ. We most move to heal the masses.

In *verse 11*, Jesus brings joy to our lives because here he tells her to go and sin no more. He says neither do I condemn thee. Oh, these are the words of the savior. The key is the woman knew her sin and that what she did was wrong but she cried out saying I am guilty and in response, the Lord said neither do I condemn thee.

Saints, we need to tell a dying world that if God has forgiven us we should forgive others as well. We need to be Christians who use the bathroom and tell others where the restroom is. We have found the spiritual restroom and it is time to show others of this great work that the Lord has done in and through our lives. To Him be glory and honor.

Not only does He say I will not condemn, He says go

and sin no more. Well, God says to all of us to leave what man has said and preach that He is alive in and through our lives. Oh, saints of God, we have something to tell the world about.

Yet our problem is that we do not tell the world of the forgiveness. We rather tell the world of the judgment. That is not what God gave to us. Not only did He give us judgment, He gave us grace. We cannot tell the world half the story. We must tell them the whole story of what the Lord has done in and through our lives. If God did two things, we need to do two things as well.

We cannot tell people half the story. We must yell out the whole story of life. Whoever we are in God, we did not get there by ourselves—it was because of Christ.

So as Christians, people see the handy work of God and not of ourselves. Let us put things in true perspective. I am not made by me, I am made by His power. This is why I must yell "I AM IN THE BATHROOM."

When we yell such then the world knows that the Holy Ghost is working on us. Yes world, I just finished coming from the bathroom. As a matter of fact, every time we read the word of God we have to go back in the bathroom again because we see more things that we need to work on.

God never stops working on us. However, when we walk around pretending to be perfect and complete, we say to the world that God stops His work instead of continuing forever.

Chief of Sinners

This is quite a troubling scripture because here is the greatest man that lived to deliver the gospel, yet he tells the world that he is chief of sinners. Its one thing to say I am a sinner but it is quite another to say I am the chief among all.

The apostle does not say he was just a sinner but that he was the chief sinner. If the apostle was able to express his sin then what is wrong with us in 2008? We need to always abhor but yet understand that sin that works in our lives. The problem is that on one hand you have people saying we are perfect and then on the other hand you have people who say we sin every day. Which one is right? I believe the apostle says it; we walk in one sin or another.

This is why we must stop the categorizing of sin. Sin is sin. All unrepented sin will bring the wrath of God but for the grace of God through Christ Jesus. Therefore, because of this we cannot hide in the bathroom to deal with our sin and then tell the world that we do not use the bathroom.

Stop the lying. We all have sin in our lives. The difference is that I trust in the Lord Jesus. I do not say I am good, I acknowledge my depravity and call on Christ who is able to do things that exceed all that one can ask or think.

The word sinner in the Greek is ham-ar-to-los. This means to be sinful. Yes, we are all sinful. There is none that is righteous. For too long people in Christ have walked like they walk on air. This is not the will of God.

We have to tell the truth and reach the lost with the gospel of a risen savior. We are sinners. I do not care how big or popular the church gets, we are all sinners saved by grace. Our works do not cover-up our sinfulness. We must keep this in mind no matter how high we may get in the Christian world. We are sinners and not only sinners but chief sinners.

Paul does not say I was, he says I am. This was a present tense cry of how the man felt about himself. He could have said I was but he said I am. When we tell people I was, we act as if we have arrived. Let me blow the trumpet and say we have not arrived. We are not even close yet. Yes, we are justified and gloried by the blood of Christ but without Him, we are sinners.

This is why the prosperity stage cries for us to go back to orthodox teaching. The gospel is not money, the gospel is Christ dying. If we do not preach that, we have nothing and are nothing. We cannot forget the shed blood of Christ.

Yet when a non-committed person turns on the TV, he or she is more likely to see a sermon on money than the work of Christ. We are sinners, brothers and sisters, saved by grace alone.

As in AA, we should say, "HI, MY NAME IS TIM, AND I AM A SINNER WHO IS SAVED BY GRACE". It would kill some people to say such a thing because no one wants to air their sins. However, baby, we are sinners in this land and we need the power of God to wipe away our sins.

Since we are formed in sin and shaped in iniquity, we all deal with sin. There is no level to sin. Ezekiel said that the soul that sinned would die. That cannot be erased out of the book. We are in need of a savior. That will never change.

And still we feel that after we are saved the process stops and Christ no longer needs to make any intercession. Again, this is not the case. Hebrews 7:25 says "… seeing He ever liveth to make intercession for them." Romans 8:34 says, "Who is He that condemned? It is Christ that died, yea rather, that is raised again, who is even at the right hand of God, who also maketh intercession for us"

Notice the two scriptures do not refer to the past tense but the present tense. He is making intercessions for us not later but NOW. Blessed be God for His love and power. He makes this intercession because in Hebrews 7:24 it declares He is our High priest forever. It is unchangeable. Well if Christ is the high priest, His primary responsibility is making intercession for our sins.

So in turn, Christ's job is not to give you a car, home, or money, His only job is to make intercession. Oh, how powerful it is to get to back to the word. If you look at to-day's church culture, we are more Dr. Phil than Jesus. We are not here to make people feel good, we are here to proclaim the gospel. However, how can we do that if we pretend to walk around without sin?

Let it ring from the heavens: we need a savior because we are sinners. The God of the Bible demands justice and because we could not reconcile on our own He sent his son Jesus the Christ. He is not our sugar daddy or pimp. He is our savior and high priest. Hebrews 3:1, 4:14,15; Hebrews 5:5,10, Hebrews 6:20, 7:26,8:1,9:7,11; 9:25, & 13:11. We must tell the world we are in the bathroom of life 24 hours a day and He is working on us. He is pruning us and making us better. Not worse but better. Thanks are to God for giving us the victory.

We cannot deny that the closer you get to Christ the more you see the spots. Our theology degrees must not make the gospel so high that not all can reach it. We must bring it down so that all can find the savior. The way to remind ourselves to bring it down is to express ourselves as sinners saved by grace.

When we see how messed up we are then we will see how great He is in and through us. We cannot look at one without looking at ourselves. We must look into our mirror and see the power of God at work in and through our lives. In addition, when we continue to do so, thus we will see the savior and not the sins of our brothers.

Perfect Church

(Information from answers.com & mb-soft/cp,/believe/txc)

Man has tried repeatedly to have a perfect life. Since Adam, man has tried to reclaim that perfect title, but without success. Since the Tower of Babel men have tried to reach God in their own way, and yes we Christians are called holy, but no man will ever be perfectly holy.

Yes, I know God calls us holy. I am not going against the scripture. Yet I maintain we will be holy to the best of our physical and sinful space suit, but no one will reach a perfection in which sin no longer abides. Sin abides in all— yes, even Christians. The key is what you do with it.

In the holiness movement, the work of sanctification is called the second work of grace. And yes, we are to be sanctified. However, some have taken this to mean we are perfect. Such is not attainable in this flesh suit. I believe only two men ever reached such a point with God that they were taken up bodily, and I speak of Enoch and Elijah. These men walked with God so well that God took them away. My point is that yes, we are called holy but we are no way like God to the point of perfect holiness.

In such a mind frame, we would be gods, which walks hand and hand with the New Age movement. We are still creatures of God. Again, this also smacks with Mormons, which says that after you die you will become a god. To take it further, if we are perfect then we are akin to Christ in deity. I am sorry to say to all that position is filled.

Now, I am not saying this gives us free license to sin because Romans 8 says no to it (sin life), but we must be realistic. As C J Mahoney said, death reminds us that we have sin. Now, if perfect people did not see death than I think we would all understand. But as far as the record shows, no one saying they were perfect ever skipped death. As Mr. Mahoney says, death derives from sin. So if you become perfect then death would have to be taken away. This is obviously not the case at all. Most importantly, when you go against nature by saying, you have no sin; you are going to go crazy.

I can tell you the people I have met who claim to be perfect or very holy were usually the maddest, bitterest, and most unloving people. Yet they said they were in God's presence ALL THE TIME. I am sorry, when you come into God's presence you should come away with love. Why? because I John says that God is love. Such claims to perfection run away from Christians in the bathroom. Therefore, when one who is sanctified comes off as perfect, they are not in God's presence because Isaiah the prophet said Woe is I for I am undone. However, many are saying look at me instead of Woe is me. Something is wrong with that picture.

Sanctification means to make holy. The Latin verb is *sanctificare*, which in turn derives from sanctus, holy plus facere, "to make". Which together means to make holy. The Greek for holy is hagasmos, made holy, or set apart.

Again, if we are perfect, why do we need I John 1:9 and James 5? James 5 says to confess our faults (sins) one to another. We cannot get over this hill in our lives. You and I are not perfect. When we call ourselves, very holy we take a page from our Catholic brothers in the theology of transubstantiation, which says in essence, we take wine and bread and call it Jesus infused.

This infusion in the Protestant church is not believed because no substance of its own metaphysics could be deemed Holy of it self. Only Christ has the honor and glory.

Christ alone was Homoousian and not Homoiousian. Christ alone was made from the same substance of God, which is why He alone is the final payment of sin. When we walk around as if we are perfect, we interject ourselves into abomination. Such thoughts are not healthy.

I am sorry, but only Jesus was able to be both God and man. Both Holy and in a fleshly body. No one has ever done it again. Again, no one has duplicated this act. Only Christ and Christ alone.

However, that has not stopped men from claiming this

title of perfect holiness. No one is perfectly holy. We are called upon to be holy but we can never be perfect in holiness. As we failed in the Tower of Babel, we fail in the tower of perfect holiness or Christianity.

Even if one stops all voluntary sin, they would still be guilty of involuntary sin. Did not David say we were ALL born in sin and shaped in iniquity? We all have this form in us and until we are reformed in the resurrection, we cannot see this transformation in our lives. In point, he was saying that we could not do things on our own but only by the power of God. For where we fall is where God takes over. Sanctification in point is the gap between how we are living and how we should be living. There will always be a gap and that gap is filled through Him alone and not our good works.

Usually with the perfect church goes a pastor who has a superiority complex. See if this sounds familiar from answers.com. *A superiority complex has behaviors related to this mechanism may include an exaggeratedly positive opinion of one's worth and abilities, unrealistically high expectations in goals and achievements for oneself and others, vanity, extravagant style in dressing (with intent of drawing attention), pride, sentimentalism and affected exaltation, snobbishness, a tendency to discredit other's opinions, forcefulness aimed at dominating those considered as weaker or less important, credulity, and others.*

God help us to never have such character flaws in our

own lives. Make no mistake; we all have flaws, but to have a flaw that is directly related to Satan (pride) is very bad indeed. Perfect churches and people deny a perfect God.

'Perfect' religious people suffer from narcissism. When you do not want to acknowledge God, you are usually trying to take His throne. When you do not see yourself as being in the bathroom, you are going down the road that is filled with the bones of men and women who thought they where perfect but in reality died without really knowing God.

Not anyone truly in God's presence will ever walk away in pride. They will never act envious because being in God's presence really shows you how badly off you are but also how blessed you are just to behold His presence.

I maintain that in this corruptible body I cannot reach true perfection. As a matter of fact, only in the resurrection according to Paul will we shrug off the diseased body to attain true maturity in God. This is supported in 1 Corinthians 15:42, 50, 53, & 54.

As stated earlier, as long as we have death we have sin in our mortal bodies. I am sorry but this is truth. Again, if one could reach perfection one would not be here on this earth. If one were perfect, medicine and science would make a pathway to that person's door for answers. However, such has not happened and will not happen because in such man would get glory.

In this 'perfect' church, we devalue the work of Christ. We say we can police ourselves. We say we can eradicate sin completely on our own. If that the case, why is Christ coming? Why does Christ intercede?

The fire of perfection started in some Methodist churches that went to some Holiness church and to some Pentecostal churches. All this made it possible for man to walk around in pride thinking he had reached perfection. However, that was not the case. Most of the times the children of the holiest people walked away because they saw no true love or joy.

The joy that they saw came from the person walking in their own pride, for they had reached the false summit of God and dared all to climb. However, this has been the problem all along; it was their own man made mountain that they were telling people to climb. In addition, even more so, after those same 'perfect' leaders died the movement stopped or splintered even the more.

Men have eisegesis instead of exegesis the text to derive this 'perfect' notion. Men have added (eisegesis) instead of drawing out (exegesis) from the holy text to add this ungodly theology. Nevertheless, men still try to scale the 'perfect' mountain to only fall back. Though they lie and tell all they are perfect privately they have fallen. Brothers and sisters, lets stop the lying. We still use the bathroom.

The Oberlin and Keswick movement have both tried to do the perfect holiness thing but failed. Most influences of perfect holiness came from *ante bellum* preachers before the civil war. In one hand, they brought needed reformation to the United States, including that of slavery and the suffrage of women, yet in their good they also brought a warped sense of holiness.

For example, an *ante bellum*, Charles Finney, expressed you could get there by God's help and your own efforts. However, my efforts never can or will get me to perfect holiness. We did not use synergism to be saved and we shall not use it to get holiness. My efforts can never equal God's holiness.

My sins make me morally broke. We do not have a pot to piss in. I am what I am by His grace. Paul reminds us of this in Philippians 3. In fact, he counted all things as null if not for God. However, in perfection you count yourself and your own actions. This must change.

Those persons of the perfect crew will have eccentric behavior patterns. Their actions will be designed to draw attention to themselves and not Christ. Our goal is Christ and not ourselves. We have not died for anyone's sins, only Christ has.

Ungodly men like Friedrich Nietzsche had this theory of perfection but in his theory, he said outright that there is no god. That is why perfection is more associated with atheism—because it tries to get to God's character either without his help or with his help. No one can reach perfect holiness. No one.

This is why the conclusion is to rest in the finished work of Christ. We have tried and failed spectacularly to reach that apex. Only with Christ alone do we stand, yet in standing we show Christians and the world that we are still in the bathroom.

Propitiation

(Information from answers.com)

This is the act of God getting his just due for the sins we have committed. The Old Testament was a bold attempt at us doing it but it did not work which is why God had to form his son and do the deed. So not only did God say justice, he turned around through his son and said redeemed.

Propitiation said that God is now pleased to redo the relationship because the penalty has been paid. We as moral men could not pay Him, but Christ did. We came to the counter without money but it was Christ who cashed the check with His own life. Through Christ, we were pardoned and through him, we are forgiven in the glory of the Father.

Again, this is the gospel; that if Christ had not died we would have received the wrath of God, which we deserved. Instead, because of the work and completeness of Christ, He does not hail down wrath but love to those who accept his son as Christ and the payment of His death.

If we do not accept the payment, then there is no remission of the sin. If we do not accept Christ, there is no other payment we can make. Jesus the Christ atoned our sins. In other words, he paid the price. In business, someone has to pay the bill. Well, Christ was the payment of sin. The payment does not include layaway or credit cards; it had to be done completely. This is why Christ is so powerful to us; because he paid the full price. We can come boldly because we have the payment of sin in life.

On the cross it was done. Why is this important as it relates to this book? Because of what Christ did we have no right to accuse others. We are here together on the same level field called sin. In addition, yes, sin separated us, but it was God's grace that brought us back. We cannot continue to cut down one another without cutting ourselves.

If God did not have the propitiation through Christ, there would be no humans. He would wipe all of us out. However, because of the work of Christ we have a chance. If we can see that, why can't we show that testimony to the world?

Yet, for people to see God and change their lives they must see us change first. Without this change in life, our preaching the gospel would be dull. In point, they need an example. Yet when you say you have no sin, you cannot relate or demonstrate an example.

Again, propitiation reduced the wrath of God upon our lives. If God did that for us, why do we not want to tell the world about the work of Christ? A direct quote from answers.com says "By expiating (removing the problem of) sin God was made propitious (favorable) to us". Therefore, if God is favorable toward me as a sinner saved by grace, how should I treat the world? Should we treat with disdain or should we treat it with the love of God? The answer is of course the latter. Because we have been forgiven, we must do the same for others.

For if we do not love and forgive, then by default we will become legalistic. We must change our mind toward the world. If not for the grace of God there go I.

I may not get any amens on what I discuss in this book, but I am not just talking to the choir. I am taking my microphone outside the church and telling a dying world that yes, despite what you see Christians are all works in process and we still use the crapper. There are 'Christians' who divorce, curse, lust, lie, emotionally attack their wives and children, overeat, have anger issues, and pride. The list goes on but we have His grace upon our lives. This is what I am trying to tell the world.

Yes, I believe in holiness but only God can sanctify; our efforts are but nothing. Only God can give me strength. When we overcome certain sins, we should not destroy another brother or sister who has not. This is not the will of God.

I am not saying that we should live our lives like everybody else. We sin and we should confess it. However, in this confession, we can reach the world. The world is not impressed by our churches and singing. What they want to see is a person who has scars and yet lives this gospel to the best of his or her ability.

Impute

Romans 4 and 8 say blessed is the man to whom the Lord will not impute sin. Impute in the Greek is Ellogeo which means reckon to one's account or lay to one's charge. This is what Christ did for us on Calvary. First, we do not save ourselves. The Bible says it is the Lord who does this. Blessed is the man that God looks over time and says we will not impute or attribute the sin to our charge.

This is important because if sin were not cleansed, the righteous would not stand. As we read, we reckon that we do nothing before or during our salvation. The hand of God does all. If we had any hand in our salvation or forgiveness of sin, then we might be tempted to take on the messiah title. However, because God does the finished work, we are not able to boast.

Since God does the work, how can we stand and point fingers at any soul? You and I are not the messiah or Causa sui. We are flawed creatures that are in need of a savior. We stand in the face of God by his grace. He imputed us;

we had nothing to do with it. The Old Testament represents how we tried and failed in this faith work. Therefore, what has Christ done? By His blood, God now has the tools to forgive sin. Without the blood of Christ, there would be no door through which for God to take us.

Therefore, since God by his son has given us His grace, what stops us from telling the world what the Lord has done? I believe the reason why we are silent is that we want the world to see us and say how glorious we are in our walk with God. Yet every walk and step is not by my own virtue but by the shed blood of Christ. I am not here because of the glory of time, I am here by the GLORY of God the Father.

In point, it is not on our account any more. God takes away our account of sin once we trust in the Lord Jesus the Christ. How powerful this is. This is why we cannot point our bony fingers at others. He has forgiven us not because of us but because of Himself. He swore by no other than Himself. In Him, I am glad and must tell the world of the good news.

By God waving his hand, I am totally and completely forgiven and my sins are placed in another area. In point, we do not have to carry the load around anymore. For too long, the church has not established that point that we do not have to carry the load. Yet some church people want to carry it and walk around as if they got it all together and have people look at them in awe and bow down. No sir and madam, we only bow to the king. We only honor the king. We only give praise to the King. Therefore, this is why we must shout to the world that God is working on us and we are not working on ourselves. He got me in the palm of His hand. He got me all hooked up and ready to go. We have our life on the potter wheel.

As we know the clay has nothing to do with His form, so neither do we. We have nothing to do with our form. We are nothing going in and we are nothing going out. We come and go by His blood. So because we are the clay and God is the potter, how dare we try to make the adjustments on our own?

How dare we try to tell others we made ourselves? How dare we walk around the church as if we got here on our own? The devil is a liar. We must tell the world we are on the toilet of life. We must let the world know that we did not make a life to marvel at. It is God and God alone who has done that.

Imagine the clay making itself. It would not happen. It could not see where it was going or what it was doing. There is no way it could have breathed life into itself. So as messed up as the clay making itself is, so is the notion that we make ourselves. We do not make ourselves. It is God and God alone. We cannot take on the title of creator. We are always the created. Yes, He created me. He is forming me into what He wants me to be.

This is why this book targets pride by letting others

know that it is God who has done this and not ourselves. When I see the power and myself in His hands then I am able to move beyond myself and see Christ. Yes, world, I am letting the cat out of the bag. We Christians are not perfect. We are only the clay and God is working on us to bring forth His glory and honor of the Son of God.

You Lazy Person

In the Catholic Church, there are seven deadly sins. One of them is sloth or (Latin) Acadia. Many Christians do not recognize this as a sin but when you know to do well and doeth it not; it is a sin. When you hold your hand back from the work that God commands, you are sinning. Many people give the excuse of being lazy and tired. When you accept your flesh reaction to the plan of God, you are in sin. This is why James 4:17 needs to be added to all of our lives as it relates to sin.

Again, the purpose of this book is to help believers understand that even if we may not do the BIG (so called) sins, we all sin and do things unpleasing to God. Being lazy is one of these things.

But here James expands our minds to understand that when you withhold good you are in sin. Knowing what to do and not doing it is a sin. You cannot run from this because God has given all of us a conscience that is directly in line with HIM.

Many persons have messed up because they refuse to get up from their spiritual sofa and do the work of the Lord. Yes, you may be tired, but the Bible says to not be weary in well doing. If you do not faint, you will have a big response down the road. There is no way you can do this on your own. There is no way you can sit back and watch either. You must press on and do the work of the ministry. Being tired does not work.

As we walk, we must remember that if God gave us the vision, he also gave the provision. If God made it happen, then it must happen and He will give us the strength to go on. If you got it, He will give you the muscle. Yes, adultery and homosexuality are sin. Laziness to the command of God lines up to adultery and homosexuality as sin as well.

In the commentary by Critical and Explanatory, overall Bible (JFB) expresses that there are nothing like wasted impressions or opportunities that the Lord will place in and around our lives. Here the Creator tells you to do, and not only has He told you to do but He has given you the strength to do. There are ramifications of inaction. This cannot be avoided. Which is why to God it is a sin. It was a sin for the people of Israel to not go into the Promised Land, but because of their lack of faith, God held back their blessing. They did not trust His word. In addition, on this journey you must trust God's word more than your own.

This again is why laziness is so abhorrent to God. When you take His word and commandment and put it under your seat and do nothing, and then you have the nerve to ask God to bless you, you are in sin. In point, when I leave this life I want to be empty. I do not want leftovers. I want God to take full control of me and whatever He placed in me; I want out of myself by the time I close my eyes. Yet many let laziness get the best of them. This is not acceptable. We all must work the work of Christ.

There are sins of omission and of commission. Laziness surely is a sin of omission. Being AWOL is equal to going to war and shooting your brother in battle. When we sit on our hands or fold our arms, we then find ourselves committing the sin of omission.

I was told to do but I omitted it from my spiritual checklist. I was told to go but I removed it from my list of things to do because I was tired. Dear sirs and madam, all are sin. When you do not do the will of God and blame it on being tired, you are guilty.

What if Annasias told God he was tired and did not go and pray for Paul? We would have a missed a large piece of the gospel. What if Philip said he was tired and had not run to the Eunuch? Then the gospel would have not spread to Africa. What if Elijah did not run to the chariot? He would have missed the boat with Ahab.

So many more people have run this race and felt tired while they ran. Therefore, for those who give up, throw in the towel, and become a pot-bellied Christian ,you are lazy and will be judged for your sins of omission and laziness.

Luke 12:47-48 tells how the servant was whipped with more stripes because he did not go into action. He did not give 100%. In other words, he was lazy. Many preachers do not give their all, depending upon the offering and crowd. Dear sir, you are in sin because you are lazy and are not giving the Bible the gospel of the Lord Jesus the Christ.

John 15:22 says in essence that when God speaks to you, you have no more justification for laziness because he told you. When you do not adhere to the word of God, you are in sin. This is especially true when God gives out a command order. You must follow that order all the way. We cannot forget we are soldiers and conquerors. We cannot forget we are called to the battleground of Christ and we cannot throw in the towel. We must continue this race until the end. We must rebuke laziness and do the will of God. Once I hear, I must obey. We cannot waver from the voice of God in these matters.

In Wikipedia, it is states that laziness is also associated with sadness. Sadness and depression can come in as the result of being lazy and not working the work of Christ. When you do not work the work, you must expect sadness to come. Our joy comes from Christ as well as because of our obedience to his will.

Also in Wikipedia, it states that laziness is manifest in not utilizing one's talent and gifts for the glory of the Lord. In addition, you withhold things that are not yours to withhold. We often forget that we are stewards. As stewards, we own nothing. However, in our modern culture, we have men who run around as if their gifts and accomplishments totally belong to them.

However, we must remember that that is not our calling. Our calling is to be stewards of what God has given in the place of talents and time. This is especially true for those who use their talents for the world but not for God. This to me magnifies the lazy spirit.

How can you say you love God but only use your talents Monday through Friday? No sir. You are lazy and such is sinful. Here, my Christians, we use the bathroom when we are lazy. When we do not get a reality check on ourselves we will fall prey to a problem of great proportions. In fact when we judge others more than ourselves, we are lazy.

Why? It is easier to judge and correct others than yourself. It easy to correct, it is harder to help. Did not Paul say to those who are strong that they should bear the infirmities of those who are weak? When we do not such, we have sinned. We cannot continue this slide. If my brother needs me and I do not come to his rescue, I am in sin. I am lazy. I am wrong. Oh people of God, we cannot continue to kill our wounded. We must correct this issue in our lives.

(used KJV and NKJV from Crosswalk.com)

Judges 18:9
    And they said, Arise, that we may go up against

them: for we have seen the land, and, behold, it is very good: and are ye still? be not **sloth**ful to go, and to enter to possess the land.

Proverbs 10:26
As vinegar to the teeth and smoke to the eyes, so is the **lazy** man to those who send him.

Proverbs 12:24
The hand of the diligent shall bear rule: but the **sloth**ful shall be under tribute.

Proverbs 12:27
The **sloth**ful man roasteth not that which he took in hunting: but the substance of a diligent man is precious.

The **lazy** man does not roast what he took in hunting, But diligence is man's precious possession.
Proverbs 13:4
The soul of a **lazy** man desires, and has nothing; But the soul of the diligent shall be made rich.

Proverbs 15:19
The way of the **sloth**ful man is as an hedge of thorns: but the way of the righteous is made plain.

The way of the **lazy** man is like a hedge of thorns, But the way of the upright is a highway.

Proverbs 18:9
He also that is **sloth**ful in his work is brother to him that is a great waster.

Proverbs 19:15
Slothfulness casteth into a deep sleep; and an

idle soul shall suffer hunger.

Proverbs 19:24
A **sloth**ful man hideth his hand in his bosom, and will not so much as bring it to his mouth again.

A **lazy** man buries his hand in the bowl, And will not so much as bring it to his mouth again.

Proverbs 20: 4
The **lazy** man will not plow because of winter; He will beg during harvest and have nothing.

Proverbs 21:25
The desire of the **sloth**ful killeth him; for his hands refuse to labour.

The desire of the **lazy** man kills him, For his hands refuse to labor.
Proverbs 22:13
The **sloth**ful man saith, There is a lion without, I shall be slain in the streets.

The **lazy** man says, "There is a lion outside! I shall be slain in the streets!"

Proverbs 24:30
I went by the field of the **sloth**ful, and by the vineyard of the man void of understanding;

I went by the field of the **lazy** man, And by the vineyard of the man devoid of understanding;

Proverbs 26:13

The **sloth**ful man saith, There is a lion in the way; a lion is in the streets.

The **lazy** man says, "There is a lion in the road! A fierce lion is in the streets!"

Proverbs 26:14

As the door turneth upon his hinges, so doth the **sloth**ful upon his bed.

As a door turns on its hinges, So does the **lazy** man on his bed.

Proverbs 26:15

The **sloth**ful hideth his hand in his bosom; it grieveth him to bring it again to his mouth.

The **lazy** man buries his hand in the bowl; It wearies him to bring it back to his mouth.

Proverbs 26:16

The **lazy** man is wiser in his own eyes than seven men who can answer sensibly.

Ecclesiastes 10:18

By much **sloth**fulness the building decayeth; and through idleness of the hands the house droppeth through.

Matthews 25:26

His lord answered and said unto him, Thou wicked and **sloth**ful servant, thou knewest that I reap where I sowed not, and gather where I have not strawed:

But his lord answered and said to him, 'You wicked and **lazy** servant, you knew that I reap where I have not sown, and gather where I have not scattered seed.

Romans 12:11

Not **sloth**ful in business; fervent in spirit; serving the Lord;

Titus 1:12

One of them, a prophet of their own, said, "Cretans are always liars, evil beasts, **lazy** gluttons."

Hebrews 6:12

That ye be not **sloth**ful, but followers of them who through faith and patience inherit the promises.

If The Lord Would Mark Iniquity

For reasons of pride and self-righteousness, many have forgotten a scripture that applies to every man and woman. If God would mark iniquity who would stand? If God would count everything that we have done, we would not be in that place of God to come boldly.

Those who have unknowingly adopted a Pelagiamism mentality of original sin foolishly believe they can make the change of good on their own. Yet any man who has examined himself knows that we stand not on our own merit but by the precious blood of the risen savior. I am not my own, I have been bought at a price.

The item being sold has no power over the one who buys it. The buyer is in control of the item. The dress, shoes, or car is in the hand of the buyer. If the buyer has the price, the item goes to the highest bidder. Well, this is what God has done. We look at our sins and if we are not careful, we think we have no mark against us. But all have sinned. All have marks against them, and only through the blood of Christ can we continue this journey with God.

This was a rhetorical question. We all know the answer to this, but it takes one who is prideful to answer wrongly. Despite our accomplishments and great feats of faith, the initial movement and continued movement of God is needed in our lives. For we must not forget it was the publican and not the Pharisees who received the praise of God. Because he understood his position.

We take orders from him; we do not give orders to him. We can only ask. He can demand. Many look at their church, pews, and TV programs and brag about how great they are, but in Zechariah, we find the high priest in his dirty clothes because he is sinful.

This book is to help Christians study other forms of sin and come before the savior with humble minds and not prideful spirits. We can all be puffy but such occasions can only hurt us in areas that will affect our walk and growth with the Lord

Psalms 53 says to all of us that there is a God and because there is a God, there is judgment. Many do not want a God because such would require justice, which brings us back to Psalms 130. We all have marks, yet when we walk around thinking that our scarlet letter is smaller than that of another, then pride will raise its head. We've got to shift and move from this place of pointing fingers, to just looking at our selves.

When one defecates, it does not matter if it is a little or a lot, it all still sinks and is dirty. Well, we must yell out to Christians everywhere to become organized and stop the pointing and thank God for His mercy and grace. Neither you nor I have done anything to deserve it. We move and have our being by his grace. Our position, titles and the admiration of men are all nothing without realizing the grace of God.

A spirit of Simony has hit our churches. This script comes from the desire to gain at any cost. It comes from having a mind frame that everything is up for sale. However, the Devil is a liar. All who are predestined have been paid for by the Blood of Christ.

The straight definition of simony is buying or selling church offices. This, friend, is Christians on the toilet. It is only the anointing that gives position. We are not super, we are only human.

There are no superstars or super apostles in God's army. In 2 Corinthians, a spirit of super apostles went through the church and I believe that same damnable spirit is within our churches now: look at my glory, look at my works, and look at my church. To me, this sounds more closely related to Satan than to the Savior. When we trust our works more than the work of the cross, we are in trouble.

Even Jesus said in John 4 verse 37 that one soweth but another reapeth. If it's God's will for you to sow then so be it. If it is God's will for you to sow and reap, it is God's will. The point being all comes from the grace of God.

He does all according to his will and not ours. God forgives the arrogant preacher that feels he can work all on his own. The devil is a liar. This is why we must let the world know that we are here by God's grace. Only God has the power. It does not fall on us but on him alone. There is but one redeemer and savior. We have no right to such titles. We walk and breathe by His will. We have nothing unless He gives it to us.

I am not my own redeemer. We cannot redeem ourselves. I am here by His grace and mercy. We have added nothing to it. We must tell the world that yes, Christians sin.

Christians who are prideful act as if they have no mistakes and no faults. However, behind that mask is sin. We have all sinned according to Romans 3, so stop fighting it and face the problem. The problem is sin, but the redeemer of the curse of the law is Christ Jesus. No other can take that title.

We cannot declare ourselves clean. As only the High Priest in the Old Testament would declare a sinner clean, so only Christ by his spirit declares God's select clean. Many are called but few are chosen.

We are chosen not because we are good but in spite of our goods and faults. Christ cleans. Christ wipes. Christ justifies. We cannot do these things on our own. We walk and live by His power, no ifs, ands, or buts about it. We have tried to clean ourselves with no avail.

As a person tries to keep his white suit clean but gets dirty in time, so is my soul dirty. We cannot keep ourselves clean. I am clean by the word of God. Point blank. We cannot do anything on our own. We walk by Him and breathe by Him.

This is the point and fact that we must carry over to a world that looks at the church and says because of my sin, the church will fall once I enter. No sir, it has not fallen; and it will not because of Christ blood and sacrifice.

We have to let the world know we are using the bathroom while preaching, singing and using our things in church. The greater sin is to not admit you have sin. Job 10:14 says that if I sin, He will mark me. What more proof do I need about myself? Every sin has a mark. Yet Christ is our advocate. He does take away our sin and in doing so, we are washed clean. I cannot look down on you because God looks down on me and sees my marks.

The Bible said blessed is the man whose sins are covered. His blood covers us. We are not covered because of our good but we are covered because of what He did on Calvary. He alone redeems. He alone saves. He alone justifies.

My soul is full of germs and it takes the savoir of the world to wash them away. As germs are always around, so is sin. No one can be totally exempted from either.

This is why in the latter portion of this book I look at the sins that are not often mentioned to show us how messed up we are without Christ. Whether good or bad, God does not discriminate between persons. He cuts both ways. Due to this, we need Christ. Not a bigger briefcase or cards, we need Him from beginning to end.

According to Drake, this is questioning 158 in which we are all looking at sin and ourselves with our marks of wrong through our lives. We are all on the same level playing field. We are on the same field of play and thank God for that.

Can you image the arrogance of people who never sinned versus those who had? The church would be messed up between the haves and have nots. Because of this we have learned to say we are all at the foot of Jesus. We all need Him from beginning to end. We cannot ever think that we have things without God in our lives. We all need Christ. We all need Him in spite of how good we are.

We must understand that we are not good within ourselves. This is why God said sin went from Adam one to Adam second, but it stopped with Jesus. From Adam to Jesus, man sinned but from Jesus to eternity we have the new creation through and by God. Without God it will not be done. God gave what we have by sacrificing His son. In addition, through His son we have life. We are saved but by his greatness. In addition, without His good, we see damnation but by God's power, we see a new movement in our lives.

When we preach, sing or dance before the people, we must see ourselves as being on the toilet because we are all being worked on. This is what the people of the world need to see and understand; that God is working on us.

In addition, when he works on us we need to let the world see us being worked on to the glory and honor of God. Hebrews 12:14 speaks of how without holiness, no man can see the Lord. Well the holiness is taken care of by the death, burial, and resurrection of Jesus the Christ.

The word of Christ is needed; we need holiness to be in good graces. Since we cannot get there on our own, we need superior righteousness to do it. We need Jesus to be our advocate to come before the throne.

Yes, we come boldly to the grace of Christ but we come not by our merits but by the shared blood of Christ. It is in Christ alone that I am holy. Not I but He has taken me from death to life.

Romans 9:15

God says in His word that He will have mercy and compassion. This is a very powerful scripture because it eliminates all of us from trying to put the final touch on who makes heaven and who makes hell.

In this book, I have tried to say that we all have sin in our lives and only God has the power of redemption. Only He can distribute grace. Mercy is not based on me or the type of church I go to. The mercy that flows from the Lord only flows from Him alone.

As there is scripture alone, Christ alone, faith alone, so there is mercy alone. A mercy that only flows down from the hand of God. We do not add or take away. There is no indulgences that we can do to add more mercy to our lives. If God does not give it, we will not function.

For some reason we forget that we live and breathe by the mercy of God. If that extends in our flesh how much more must it extend in our spirit? Our souls are depraved. We cannot do anything on our own to wipe away the sin that is in our lives. We hear Isaiah 1: 18 say come now let us reason together. God said that He ALONE cleans and redeems. Nowhere in this text do we hear how man helps God. If man could help God, there would be no Christ. Yet because men failed repeatedly, not only did the justice of God rain down but also God had to create a plan for salvation. Nothing in myself can deliver me from sin. It is like being in a hole and expecting to get out of it by one self. Our own proclivity has made us understand that we have this nature of sinning and we cannot help it.

Proclivities are things that are in our nature. Due to this we as Christians must constantly fight a feeling that we must constantly fight the things that we desire to do. We do not recognize the sins in our own lives. We love to point but not at our ourselves , only at others.

If I am in trouble, it will take another person to get me out. My sins are so messed up, it will take a superior spirit to deliver me from the sin that I have in my life. This is why the scripture says that all have sinned and are short of the glory of God.

Which means that we have worked so hard on things and yet have come up short. We have done all the merit and assistance with God and it still has not helped. This is why again we have Romans 9:15. Romans 9:15 tells us without question that it is God who does these things. If God does not give mercy, then there is no mercy. Yet if God gives mercy but we do not give mercy His mercy overrules mine.

If I give mercy but God decides not to give it, than Coram Deo. We cannot fight against what God wants to do.

All is in God. Notice in the sentence that I am not mentioned, but only God's power. For reasons of pride, we think we have the market cornered on who will be blessed and who will be extended the love of God. However, if we look over our lives, it was not us who choose God but God Himself.

The word of God said that while we were yet sinners, Christ died. While I was on the toilet, God was dying on the cross for me. In this point, we have no power to beat down another person. How dare I try to hurt another person, how dare I mess up another person's spirit?

We cannot point to another sin without first looking at our own lives. The law was given to know that we have sin. Without law, we would not understand that we have transgressed, yet Jesus not only shows justice but it also shows the power of God to forgive and grant forgiveness.

I am stressing Christ because until we see Christ alone we will see only ourselves instead. In addition, it was not us who gave us the power to live this thing. In fact, it was us who brought Jesus to the earth to die for our sins. It took an outside source to save me from my wrongs. It took God's hand to move me from to the right. However, it is not my righteousness but His alone.

This passage comes from Exodus 33:19 when God spoke to Moses and showed him His glory. Now, it was a death sentence to see the glory of the Lord, but again, God gave mercy. We must not think that there are any people that God cannot save.

If God saved you and me, what stops him from saving other people? I say this because we look at people's sins and say they are beyond hope. However, you and I were not beyond hope. If God saved us, he can save others. There is no sin that God cannot bring one up from.

This grace and mercy reminds us that we are in the bathroom. It reminds us that God was the one to lift me from my sin. I had absolutely nothing to do with it, yet when we walk around as if we did saves ourselves, we act self-righteous. We do not acknowledge that we use the spiritual bathroom.

The point is that you must understand that your sin is no bigger or smaller than that of the next person. We all have sin that reigns in our mortal bodies. We cannot say that our neighbor is doing something that we have not done ourselves. We are all on a level playing field. We must expect this and be blessed for what the Lord has provided.

If we look at this text a little harder, we will see the power of God's mercy upon our lives. In the text, it says that despite the sin and rags of Moses, He let him pass before him. His glory should have killed or hurt Moses. God could have chosen to pass His judgment on Moses. However, He chose goodness.

He does not pass His goodness because of our goodness.

Our goodness can in no way compare to His goodness. So in point, he has given us goodness in spite of our badness. So why do I not give God the glory for who and what I am?

Since the degree of God's goodness upon my life is so great, why do I not give my grace to others as well? When we see this power of God upon our lives, we cannot condemn. We should be so into thanking God we would not have time to fuss or cut another believer. Our time should be spent in telling the world 'look what the Lord has done'.

In spite of my sins and wrongs, He has passed goodness. Looking over my sins and wrongs, He has given out love and not judgment to me by His own will and plan. We had nothing to do with it. Therefore, if he gives me love I thank him. If he gives me judgment, we thank him because the Lord is good and just. Just means he knows how to cut right according to His will. Even when we think God is wrong, He is right.

He gives me good despite the crap within me. God's mercy is enough to esteem His greatness.

God is sovereign and He does only what He wants to do. If He does not want to do it, then it will not be done. We must dig deep and believe that He has His plan and role in our lives and yes, we have no choice but to accept what God wants.

Again, God has the right to choose and what He wants. God is right in all things. There is no shadow of sin or wrong judgment. Therefore, if God chooses one over another, He is sovereign and righteous. The reason why this scripture is so powerful is because it reminds us to not look down on other people. It is only by His graces that we move and have things.

We can never forget that it was God's opinion and not our own. He chose us, we did not choose him. The Bible declares that unless the spirit draws, no one can come. No one can enter. So how can I hurt another brother or sister because they wrestle with a sin? We all use the same bathroom. No one is perfect or correct. Only God chooses what and whom He wants. We may not like this point but it is His world and not ours.

We are made according to His purpose and not our own. This gain is why the scriptures in the latter part of this book will hopeful challenge us in ways we have not been challenged before. We pray that it helps us see ourselves instead of our brother or sister.

By our own arrogance, we forget that we are the creature and not the Creator. In other words, God directs us, we do not direct Him. In point, we must look on each other and see the favor of God and how He has shined on all who call themselves of the household of faith. Nothing you or I have done anything ourselves; we breathe and move by His power. Nothing more or less.

Lamentations 3:21-23

We are in this race because of God's mercy. That is not just new upon conversion but new every morning. The book of Lamentations speaks of the prophet Jeremiah pouring out his heart to God. Due to the sins of Israel, God saw his people shipped into captivity.

Yet in the midst of the pain, he had to remind himself of something. It was not riches or glory that he had to remind himself of. It was God's mercy. In the body of Christ, we must do the same. We cannot be so caught up in our Christian amour that we forget that we have what we have by His mercy. Mercy that is not only applied once but that is applied on a daily basis.

When Christians do not remember how God has brought them up, they become arrogant and judgmental of others. They forget that they are on the toilet as well. All is not well in the garden of our Eden. We all must keep this in mind. We cannot act as if we have it on our own.

Due to the size and popularity of Christianity in certain

areas, we forget that if not for God's mercies we would be consumed. Can you take this picture to heart? If God did not give us new mercies daily, we would be consumed. As we know that our atmosphere blocks the rays of the sun, so does God's mercy keeping us from God's own judgment.

Oh how powerful is the love of God. In one moment, He calls for death but in the same breath He calls for mercy. This again is why we must stop the pointing of the fingers. We are all under the umbrella of God's mercy. Yes, even the sinner is covered.

Why? If they were not covered, wicked people would be destroyed like crazy. However, that doesn't happen. His mercy and grace shines on who He wants it to shine on. I must say, Christians we should not beat our breasts with pride, we instead should bow before the savior and say thank you God for sharing your mercy.

If God can share his mercy with me, why do I not share it toward foe and friend? The world's problem with Christians is that we act as if we are perfect and all is well. We Christians act as if we have no sin after conversion. Yet in my book, saying you have arrived or are better than another denies the need of the toilet. We must let others know that we are no better. We are here by His glory in this life.

In Jeremiah's words, great is God's faithfulness. There is no time and power to really understand this statement but it is true. We are here because when we were not faithful to God He was faithful to us.

So why can we not learn from this point? Because God has been faithful to us, we must learn this lesson and be faithful to others. We must take the same patience of life and apply it toward others.

We are so impatient with people. Yet in our sins, God is ever faithful, so what is our problem? We want to quickly condemn all to hell. We want a spiritual monopoly. Did not God give us patience? Is not God faithful toward us? I am sorry but if we continue to condemn, our churches will become gang dens and mafia hide outs. We will do more for the dark than the light. We will be known more for legalism than the power of the word of God. It's time for *Post Tenebras Lux*.

It's time for "After the Darkness, Comes the Light". Saints of the highest God, we have been in darkness long enough. We have not used the light of the world, which is Jesus the Christ. In fact, we have been guilty of adding to the darkness rather than exposing the light because of our envy and strife. That is not how God deals with us, if God gives us mercy then what is our problem in giving other people mercy? We must wake up from this nightmare.

As God's love is not based on what we do or do not do, we should follow suit. We should not love people based on what they have or have not done. We must love no matter what. We must turn from our wicked ways and love anyway. We cannot find a substitute for this. In fact, we cannot be forgiven unless we forgive.

Cynics & Epicureans

(Info from answers.com & religionfacts.com)

Philosophy comes in when there is the absence of God. When God is not there, man will put himself on that throne. When we walk around like we got it going on and things are being done without God's mercy, we are verging on philosophy without God.

Those who act as if they do not use a toilet are not following the gospel of Christ. Christ said take up your cross and follow me. Christ said forgive others if you want to be forgiven. Well we say to all, when you criticize other people for something you yourself do in private you are not a Christian but a philosopher who does not believe in his or her own thinking. Yet when we walk around under the banner of grace, we have something to be happy for.

When you give quick judgment, you are not saved. When you gossip you are not saved. When you tear down you are not saved. When you have no compassion you are not saved. When you have no fruit of the spirit you are a philosophy major of self and not a disciple of God.

We are not living this journey on our own. We are not walking based on how good we are. We stand on the work of Christ. When we portray that we are perfect and do not use the toilet of life. we tell God that the work of Christ was not needed or necessary.

This is true especially when we destroy others for title and gain. We have to move from this toward God. Once we move from old to new, then we will be what God wants, which is a creature that understands his creator.

Epicureans had a goal of luxury and the pursuit of sensual pleasure, i.e. food. If you look at the landscape, too many Christians are saying look at my gold, jet, and clothes. These things tell me how blessed and rich I am. However, this is not so. This is a western way of thinking. I am not blessed because of what I have. I am blessed because my name is written in the lamb's book of life.

Epicurus (341 to 270 B C) founded epicureans. If they had a theme, it was to eat, drink and be merry. Sometimes that seems to be the rally cry of Christians today. Sometimes we act like we got in and so to hell goes the world. However, this is not the will of God.

The will of God is to show love to all. People forget that Job had to pray for his enemies. After he prayed, things turned around. We must do the same if we expect a change in our lives.

The Epicureans did not deal with the public. They

wanted to be kept apart from everyone. They wanted to be segregated. Again, this type of thinking has entered into the body of Christ. The body of Christ is love but it seems we are destroying one another while we hide under a rock from the world. It's like we are spiritual assassins to all that will not believe in the way we do. There is no more praying for one another. There is no repenting, just hate. We must make the change.

What I just mentioned is happening every day in the body of Christ. We must be turned from this. We must be honest and say we have been on the toilet. When we walk in disagreement and make others the enemy, something is wrong. We all must change.

Cynics were Greeks that believed in poverty and wanted to suppress desires. This sounds like Christianity but the Cynics did not believe in God. We have such yet in our churches. We have Christians who know how to suppress their desires but are mean like the devil. The know how to say no to their flesh. They know how to fight off sexual desires but they are mean like the devil. They cannot show any love or emotion that is great toward anybody. Yes, they know how to control their bodies but all things are wrong. They want heaven but they hate the creatures of God. This book will help us find and look at ourselves.

What good is it to control your flesh but hate people? You have not love or remorse for people when they fall. When you fall, you want all to forgive but when others fall there is no forgiveness at all. There is no love. We immediately want the death penalty. We immediately gossip instead of pray. We sit in churches gossiping and hating while praising God from the same tongue. This is not the will of God. Yes, the cynics controlled their flesh, but they still had lost the perspective of God. I believe many in the house of God have done the same.

Let a brother fall and we want death but when we fall, we want another chance. Why do we do such? Why are we impatient toward other people but we want patience and love for ourselves? God help us. It seems like the Cynics performed before people and showed them their power to withhold or sustain (sanctify). Does this sound like Christians today who walk around with big Bibles and jewelry but no big love?

They know on whom to prophecy damnation but when they fall they want mercy or they justify their sin. We must take a turn. We must seek the Lord. We must admit our issues and sins to help the world know that we are just sinners who are saved by grace. Again, the Cynics mastered their desires and needs. Sometimes people will brag about how they control their flesh. Yes, the Bible says to control our flesh, but when you do it with a mean spirit toward others you will not be blessed.

How can you move from hell to heaven and not love people? How can you have no patience for people? As the Cynics, some Christians parade their poverty and suppression of desires. The Cynics also had indifference toward others. They had to have this high and mighty spirit. They wanted to lord over people with their works. Again, this should ring familiar of Christians who walk around as if they have every answer. They have everything that they need.

They go on, gossip, and hate people when they do not get their way. Sirs and madam this is not the will of God in any way. How can you say you love God and still hate your brother? How can you say you are anointed but cannot anoint the wounds of those who were in battle? I do not understand these Christians. You cannot continue in this vein. We cannot be happy with that mind frame. Oh yes, even Christians use the bathroom and may I say we back up the toilet with our mess and hatred toward each other and the world.

Cynics would evangelize, watch humanity, and hound people for the errors of their ways. Does not this sound familiar to some big time Christians who walk around with those same three issues? They evangelize but it is not the gospel of Christ, it is their own gospel. They want people to come to them and not to Christ. This shows us that they have power but not knowledge. They know how to preach but they preach their own gospel. They make disciples after them and not after Christ.

They only know truth for themselves. Catch you in a sin, they criticize you. Yet if they have done the same sin, they justify it or outright lie about it with no remorse at all. Something is wrong with this picture. It is as if they have a postmodern mentality toward truth. Truth is defined by them and not by the Bible.

We must all be careful of such spirits. They are people who watchdog humanity. Again, this sounds so familiar. They know how to say others are wrong but they cannot see their own sins. They degrade people for moral sins but they are on their fifth divorce and yet have fornication. Something is wrong with this plot.

There is no more time for us to know other people's sins and not our own. We must make a change. We must make a change so that people will not see us in the light of a witch-hunt. It is like some Christians want to do nothing but point out sin unless it is their own. They show no compassion or love, just total judgment. They want to be judge, lawyer, jury and executioner.

Oh, God help us to see our sins. Help us God to be salt and not just hot pepper. Yes, we are to point out the sins of others, but if is not done with compassion or love how can we make it? How can we really evangelize the world?

We know every sin but we see no sin in our own lives. We must move on from this point in our lives. We most rebuke the deceit in our lives. Too many souls are missing out because we are not showing them Christ. In point, we are showing them ourselves.

Diogenes of Sinope was a great influencer of the Cynics. He had a messiah complex. We again have Christians like that who are not humble at all. No feet washing or stewardship toward one another. I even believe that having a constantly austere look is sinful. When you look mean and stern you are not really showing the life of Christ. An austere look does not make you holy at all. The world sees a church full of stern looking people but they need to see the love. Even among ourselves, we need to show love and exhibit a smile. If we cannot show love for each other how can we show love toward the world?

We are not *Causa sui* (latin for cause itself) beings <wikepedia.com>. Only God caused Himself. I talked about *Causa sui* because the way we act, we give off an air that we have all things together. No, only God is a self-made and perfect being. We are the creation and He is the Creator or *Causa sui* because He did it himself.

Acts 24:16

I first heard these words from John Macarthur and I was cut to the core because my heart is not clear all the time.

In my mind, the key word is conscience. In point, we must be true to our heart and know what God is telling us to do. All over the world people are being moved more by opinion than the heart of God.

I cannot lift myself to be great, but I must lift myself up to be humble before the Lord. Here is Paul telling Governor Felix that he wanted a clear conscience before him and God. I believe we as men and women of God stand before Felix and pray that we have a clear conscience. When we speak of conscience we speak of the inside things. Why? Because the inside is more important than the outside. Because whatever is on the inside will come out on the outside.

This only works one way. The outside does not control the inside. However, the inside controls the outside. We must be careful that we are not so into our outside adornments that we see them as our salvation. How we beautify our church and clothes is sometimes more important to us than God. We must change such.

The reason why we are Christians on the toilet is because God is constantly working on our insides and getting rid of the stuff that causes us to not be what God wants us to be. We are on the toilet because we've got things in us that need to come up. In addition, God is always working on us to get those things out of us. However, it starts with our minds. It starts with our conscience. As Paul said, I wanted to be clean from God and man is the key to a balanced life.

If we are going to live a good life, we must let the world know that our heart is right toward it. We cannot continue to hide our hearts from things that we hate or despise about our brothers or sisters. If we smile but hold hate in our hearts, than we are living dishonestly. This is not the way God wants it. Paul wanted a clean conscience and so should we.

Paul's key was that his words were not just spoken of a clear mind but to exercise it. We cannot go into it again, but we have to avoid becoming lazy in our clear conscience. We must constantly and continually work away the shame. We must constantly work away the mess that is in our lives.

Which again tells us why Christians should be on the toilet a lot to get that stuff out of them. We must remove these things from our lives. However, we must exercise.

We must work on these things continually. We cannot take a break from clearing our conscience. When we take a break, we allow the enemy to take over. So in essence, if we do not continue to work on what is in our minds, eventually it will move from our minds to our hearts to our tongues.

Do not fool yourself; the longer you take to clear the air the heavier the atmosphere will be. In addition, if you continue to not clear the air you will lose sight of what and where you need to go. We all need to bear fruit and repent and if we do, God will clear up the things in our lives.

Dr. R C Sprout Jr. talks to us about raising our kids. He says that the number one reason why kids from Christian homes do not come to faith is that they do not see a clear conscience within the hearts and minds of their parents.

We all need to see that the most difficult people to reach will be our own families. We cannot be Billy Graham outside and not Billy Graham at home. God help us to see that a clear conscience is not outside but starts in the home. If we do not start in the home, we will not end up reaching the world.

Dr. R C. Sproul Jr. tells us that our moral authority does not make us better than our children, but it should make us humble before the Lord.

May I make a bold statement to say that maybe the highest number of sinners in the world comes from church homes? God help us. They come because they have not seen the clear conscience in our lives. Do they see a change of mind or change of attitude? God help us to keep the commitment to not just save the word but also save our homes.

Evil is Present

The apostle Paul says he has evil in him. This very point comes from Romans (7:21) which says 'I find then a law, that, when I would do good, evil is present with me'. This word evil comes from the Greek *kako's* which means worthless, depraved, injurious, bad, harm, ill, and wicked.

In the 45 times, that evil appears in the Pauline Epistles (including Hebrews) the major use is the Greek word *kako's* for evil. The other two forms of Greek are *po' nero's* and *faulo's*. *Po' nero's* means evil effect and influence while *kako's* means essentially the character. *Faulo's* means foul or figuratively wicked.

Faulo's evil appears in Titus 2:8 while 11 occurrences of *po' nero's* appear in Romans 12:9, Galatians 1:4, Ephesians 5:16, 6:13, 1 Thessolians 5:22, 2 Thessonsians 3:3, 1 Timothy 6:4, 2 Timothy 3:13, 2 Timothy 4:18, Hebrews 3:12 and 10:22.

However, the evil translation in Paul's Romans 7:21 is of his character or a part of his fabric (*kako's*). This is the stuff that is a part of him. The following are sample scriptures that deal with this form of evil:

Romans (1:30) Backbiters, haters of God, despiteful, proud, boasters, inventors of evil things, disobedient to parents,

Romans (9:11) (For the children being not yet born, neither having done any good or evil, that the purpose of God according to election might stand, not of works, but of him that calleth;)

Romans (12:17) Recompense to no man evil for evil. Provide things honest in the sight of all men

Romans (12:21) Be not overcome of evil, but overcome evil with good.

1 Corintians (10:6) Now these things were our examples, to the intent we should not lust after evil things, as they also lusted.

1 Corintians (13:5) Doth not behave itself unseemly, seeketh not her own, is not easily provoked, thinketh no evil;

1 Cor (15:33) Be not deceived: evil communications corrupt good manners

2 Corinthiaans (13:7) Now I pray to God that ye do no evil; not that we should appear approved, but that ye should do that which is honest, though we be as reprobates

Philippians (3:2) Beware of dogs, beware of evil

workers, beware of the concision.

Colossians (3:5) Mortify therefore your members which are upon the earth; fornication, uncleanness, inordinate affection, evil concupiscence, and covetousness, which is idolatry

1 Timothy (6:10) For the love of money is the root of all evil: which while some coveted after, they have erred from the faith, and pierced themselves through with many sorrows

2 Timothy (4:14) Alexander the coppersmith did me much evil: the Lord reward him according to his works:

Paul says to us that in spite of our good works we have evil present within us. This is why Paul tells us that he wants to do good but evil is present in him. Well if evil lived in Paul what about you and me? We too wrestle with this duality.

In mentioning of the scriptures above, I am trying to highlight that within us we have evil, before and after conversion. We have this continued wrestle-mania to do the right thing. But do not get it twisted; while you walk around with your head up, evil is yet waiting to come out and launch on to you.

Despite your titles, degrees, or position in life, evil is present. We may wonder why Paul did not just say sin rather than calling it evil. Sin is a nicer word but I believe Paul wanted us to look at the brevity of the issue. We look at Hitler and Judas and call them evil without a stutter at all. Yet we are in the same boat. The only issue of evil is whether you let it play out to the fullest in your life. Again, this is why we Christians still use the bathroom, because we have evil in us.

I want this to hit home—we must fight any self-righteous spirit; we do not just have sin we have evil within us. And if we fail to recognize the elephant, the elephant will kill us by either suffocation or by sitting on us. Too many times, we hear the good things about us in church and yes, that has its place and time, but in all we are still sinners.

There is a phase called smelling yourself. This is a reference to when a teenager starts to take authority when he has no authority. Well, there are Christians who have not just fooled themselves but the world into thinking that they have all their ducks in the row. No sir or madam we have nothing but CHRIST.

If not for Christ's blood, we would have nothing. Yet, this book will help remind Christians of the fact that we are no good but will also tell unbelievers in our camp who have been putting on a show that you were not invited to. That is the show of true perfection and it is not the case. We are here by His grace alone.

And yes inside of all of us is *The Strange Case of Dr. Jekyll and Mr. Hyde*. This novel by Robert Louis Stevenson shows the contract that is within every Christian. Please, I am not saying all unbelievers have Mr. Hyde in them, but we as Christians are constantly fighting this evil personality inside of us.

The novel came out in 1886 in Great Britain and was unbelievably surreal because all can identify with the community face and the secret face. In point, we should have the same face no matter what but due to evil, the fight is within. It begins with the question should I do right in public but in secret be as evil as possible.

God help us all to reconcile these ends of the spectrum. God help us as Christians to admit when our private face does not line up with our public face. We all have those issues in our lives. We curse our kids but praise them in public. We read the Bible but have lustful thoughts in our minds. This is a fight that we must fight within ourselves and not be afraid to show to the outside world.

Again, I am not saying to air your laundry for all to see, but I am also not saying you cannot walk around with an air of always clean sheets in your house. No one has continually clean sheets; we thank God for the washer and dryer. And all I am saying is that we have a washer and dryer in the precious sacrifice of Jesus Christ the son of the living God.

The novel of *The Strange Case of Dr. Jekyll and Mr. Hyde* is based a man who has living a double life. This is according to answers.com. In point, he shows how man fails to destroy all forms of evil (sin) within his life. We cannot do it. The flesh suit does not and will not ever come off. It's eternally attached until we see glory.

The novel, as with Paul, looks at Dr. Henry Jekyll as he attempts to get the evil out. Paul tried and failed. John the Baptist tried and failed. Jesus never had the problem because He was sinless. He was sinless because He was preparing to be the final sacrifice for the sins of man.

Dr. Henry Jekyll as well as others do not know how to get rid of the guilt. This is one of the great banners of Christianity versus other religions. We have a solution to our sins. We get rid of our guilt by Christ. But if we walk around like we have no guilt, our guilt stands.

Man for ages has tried to do this trick but it just does not work; we will always have sin. You and I cannot remove it. It will not work. We cannot take out something that is a part of our spiritual DNA. We are evil people.

Our minds can go north, south, east and west in the blink of an eye. This is why Christ is the only answer— because He is the one who can take away our sins and intercede for us after we sin. My works in no way take away the scarlet pain, only Christ. This is why we are Christians who still use the toilet.

Back to the novel, we all have Henry and Edward in side of us. Galatians chapter five points that out. We all have this internal struggle and for us to lie about it cancels our Christianity card. For us to throw stones without the love of God is downright evil within itself. However, the question that we all must answer eventually is: will I admit my guilt or run as if I have none at all?

The ending of the novel is that Mr. Edward Hyde kills himself and leaves a letter for Attorney Utterson and Dr. Jekyll's butler. I am not in any way advocating such. I do not want any to take this book as a point of suicide. In the novel, Mr. Hyde went mad because he tried to do something that was impossible.

Many Christians around the world go "mad" because they are trying to take something out of them that they cannot remove. No one can remove sin but by the blood of Jesus. No one has that power or authority. However, some men and women have not come to that conclusion. In fact, they run harder toward perfection. The run toward a goal that they will never attain in their lifetime. The only goal that we should be running toward should be Christ the holy one of Israel.

The word present in Romans 7:21 is *parakeimai* in the Greek, which means to lie near. This is nothing Paul had from afar. This evil that we fight within our very soul lies very near to us always waiting to take us off guard.

The NIV says that when I want to do good evil is right there with me. In every decision that I make and every thought that I have, there is evil present in me. This explains why one can have a good fast and prayer day but evil remains. How powerful this scripture says to us that evil is there.

Yes, we all will be tempted but the outcome of the

temptation is up to you and me. In point, Paul was talking about the legalism of the law. The law tells us we have sin, but just following all the commands of the law or following what is wrong is not enough because in spite of all the good that you do, evil is there. It cannot be washed away. It is there until eternity.

Some may say since it is there why fight it. Simply because we are commanded to wrestle. We are command to fight the good fight of faith. We are commanded to do this dance of life. And when we do this dance, we should let the world know that we do not have all. All that we have is in Christ.

This verse alone strikes at the heart of self-righteousness. When you look at this passage, there is no room for the criticism of a believer or non-believer. Since we have sin or evil, we need something to clean the sin. That cleaning agent is Christ the Lord. God demands justice so he must have it. He sees sin, he yells justice and only his son answers the call and gives deliverance to all who believe.

Repeatedly we are reminded in sacred scripture of the importance of this battle that is within. The time does not dictate to cover Romans 7:18 which says (NIV) "I know that nothing good lives in me, that is, in my sinful nature. For I have the desire to do what is good, but I cannot carry it out".

Briefly, Paul tells us of the plight of man that there is

nothing good inside of him. Man will always need help because of the sin of Adam. What is the answer to Paul and humankind's dilemma? What is the answer for Mr. Hyde? What can give us the hope of this evil that lays dormant within but is always ready to act? What can wash away my sins?

The answer lays in verse 24 and 25 of the eighth chapter of Romans:

> 24(NIV) What a wretched man I am! Who will rescue me from this body of death?_25Thanks be to God—through Jesus Christ our Lord!

So then, I myself in my mind am a slave to God's law, but in my sinful nature a slave to the law of sin.

Words To Challenge Us

The following words are given to challenge not just our walk with God but how we walk with our fellow man. In many books, we read and there are no applications of the ideas mentioned. I pray the following pages will ignite you to examine yourself daily to see if these sins or character points are within you.

The good character points like love, you want to be there in spite of people. Other character points like pride ought to be rebuked.

As mentioned throughout this book, we Christians have for too long categorized sin into big and small but there is no such thing with God. We have focused so much on alcoholism and fornication that we have forgotten the other sins.

The Bible still says that a little leaven is all that it takes to create a lump. Well just like cancer starts small and spreads, so has the spirit of untold or unnoticed sins spread more so in the body of Christ than those who do not know God.

Those who will be honest will agree that some Christians have been shamed by the love of unbelievers. We have to turn that ship around. We cannot continue on that road.

So again, use the reminder of the book to meditate and write down notes concerning the word and the scripture reference. I will provide room as well for you to add your own scripture and comments. If we would concentrate on the words to follow, we would not have time to judge one another.

If you dare to take the step of first finding the word and studying the scripture, I believe it will help you deal with the second command of loving your neighbor. We as Christians know how to love God but I think we have missed the mark in loving our neighbor as ourselves. The following words will challenge those points.

We can get our praise on in a second but to get our love on is another matter. To get our forgiveness on is another matter. We would rather hate and have strife than love and get things in order. We have to change this mode. We've got to change this way of thinking. I pray this book will do that.

As a pastor, I have had to constantly look at myself. Not just for lust issues, as I am a man, but for the underlying things that cause me to lose my way. As John Piper says, the underlying thing that starts sin is disbelief. We have to believe God can change not just my brother's heart but my heart. We must believe that God can turn that corner for us.

In the body of Christ, we pray for other people to change, but I think it's time for us to worship God and pray for our own issues. The puritans had it right but it changed in that they became self-righteous. Self-righteousness cannot enter if you are reading the following scriptures with yourself in mind.

Only when you realize that they are very depraved will you see yourself in another light. As long as you look in my room, you will never see yourself. As long as you see my sin, you will never see your own.

A good example of this is when one says he is moral but he has had five divorces and cheated on two of them. Morality is not just in one area sir, it is in every area of your life. My solutions are just to throw yourself on the mercy of God's court and cry out to him as a sinner. Many in our pulpits cry out to say they are a perfect example of the Bible.

I will not say that. Yes, I am a preacher but I am a preacher who is saved by grace who still messes up and sins. But the grace of God that he has given me I give to another. This is the point that the world is looking for. The world is looking for real people.

Philippians 2:15 says that we ought to be lights in a crooked and perverse nation. We cannot be dark and then expect light from the life that we live. We must appear as lights. We must appear as a light to a dying world. In addition, the best way is to let the world know that we are not perfect but God is working on us to bring about a change in our lives.

The word blameless in Philippians 2:15 in Greek is *amemptos*, which means blameless. In my mind, it does not mean perfect but in fact, it means that when we do wrong, we must go to our brothers first before they come to us.

Once we find ourselves in the wrong, I do not have to wait for Him to come. If I want to be blameless when I find myself in the wrong, I must go to my brother and sister and confess my sins. In addition, this starts in the home. It starts with me saying I am wrong to my wife and children.

When I confess my sins, I become a better man by the gospel. When I confess I tell the world that I am still on the toilet and God is working on me so that I can be blameless and strong before him.

We do not want Deuteronomy 32:5 on us where God calls his nation perverse and crooked, but if we do not continue to love and forgive one another than we will become just that. We will have the curse on our lives that we are not in command of God's word.

We cannot continue to hate one another and the world as well. There is no way such actions will go unheard or unrebuked. We must understand this. The world is tired of phonies and hypocrites in the church. We have to tell the world that we are on the toilet too. We have to tell the world that faith without works is dead. In addition, when we speak of works, we speak in reference to our fellow man.

We all know how to love God. We all know whom to worship but we have to crack this code of loving our brother. The splits and infighting in the body of Christ proves without a doubt that we have a long way to go. We Christians should be the example of getting things right but in turn we get things wrong.

I believe we all have to be converted. Jesus said that to Peter. When you are converted, the world comes from stref-o which means to twist quite around. When He spoke this in Luke 22, He was trying to get Peter to understand that we cannot help our brothers until we are converted.

It may be that that is the problem that plagues us. We have unconverted people strengthen the brothers. In fact, you have broken people trying to help those who are still broke. I am not saying that we are perfect because we are not but people appreciate honesty. People appreciate when you tell the truth about yourself. People do not like those who just point. They like those who will speak the truth even if the truth is about someone in high authority.

We all sin even after being saved. This is why "Even Christians use the Bathroom" was written. We use the bathroom because I am yet a sinner in a need of a God and savoir.

Minister Al Johnson of Restoration Springs Interdenominational Church asked in a prayer service: when people devour and cut you what comes out of you? He spoke of bitterness and love; envy and power; revenge and kindness.

When he said that he hit the nail right on the head. Oh, God, we want people to see You in us, especially when they devour or speak evil of us. This is a test that only you know that you passed or failed. When people keep biting and attacking, what are they tasting?

If it is not God then something is very wrong. We cannot be Christian without the love of God in our lives, and the love is only tested when people attack or persuade us. This is even true when they give constructive criticism toward us; how do we react? Do we react in a judgmental way or do we respond with love and power?

Someone said that the church is full of wounded soldiers and many times the wounds come from people within the church and not outside the church. This is an assessment that all of us must take on. It will come. Those strong and sometimes true words will hit you. Sometimes strong and spiritual words will come at you. They may yell at you and call you all types of things but you and I must know the word of the Lord. That word is to let joy abide. Let power abide.

Let not confusion be the last word in your life. Let not bitterness be the taste of those who come after you whether in or out of the church. We want the power of God to be the taste of the day. We want God on the menu. God help us.

Lastly, do not look at others, keep the mirror on yourself.

A

Accuse, False
A strong feeling of displeasure or hostility.

2 Samuel 3:7
Psalms 35: 11 -13
Psalms 109: 6-7
Psalms 120: 2-3
Matthew 12:10
Matthew 27:12
Mark 15:3
Luke 11:54
Luke 23:10
John 8:6, 10
Acts 23:30
2 Timothy 3:3
Titus 2:3
Revelations 12:10

Anger
A strong feeling of displeasure or hostility.

Psalms 27: 9-10
Psalms 30: 5
Psalms 37: 8
Psalms 77: 9
Psalms 78: 38
Psalms 85: 5
Psalms 103: 8
Psalms 103: 8
Psalms 145: 8 - 9
Matthew 5:2
Mark 3:5
Mark 6:19
Luke 15:28

Acts 7:9
Acts 17:16
Acts 23:7
Galatians 5:20
Ephesians 4:26
Ephesians 4:31
Ephesians 6:4
Colossians 3:8
Colossians 3:21
1 Timothy 2:8
Titus 1:7
James 1:19
James 4:2

Animosity
Acts 12:20
Ephesians 4:31

Assist
To give help or support to, especially as a subordinate or supplement; aid

2 Kings 6:22
Psalms 16: 15
Psalms 40: 13
Matthew 10.8
Acts 9:27
Acts 18:24-26
Romans 15:1-3 (strong ought to bear)
James 2.15-17
1 Corinthians 10.24
1 Corinthians 10.33
Philippians 1:19
1 Thessalonians 5:12-15
1 John 3.17
1 John 5:16

163

B

Bitterness
Marked by resentment or cynicism

Psalms 64: 3
Psalms 69: 21
Matthew 5:21-25 (angry gift)
Matthew 6.12,14,15
Matthew 13.58
Matthew15.11
Romans 3:13-19
1 Corinthians 1:10-16
1 Corinthians 3:3-5
Ephesians 4:31
Philippians 2:3, 14
Colossians 3:13
Colossians 3:19
Hebrews 12.15 (root of)
James 3.14-16

Boasting
To glorify oneself in speech; talk in a self-admiring way

Psalms 5: 5
Psalms 10: 3
Psalms 12: 3
Psalms 20: 7
Psalms 34: 2
Psalms 38: 16
Psalms 44: 8
Psalms 52: 1
Psalms 94: 4
Psalms 97: 7
2 Samuel 15:2
Matthew 6:6

Matthew 7:1-5
Matthew 20.26
John 9:34
Romans 12:16
1 Corinthians 4.6
1 Corinthians 13.4
James 4.16
1 Peter 2.1
2 Peter 2.19
Jude 1:16

Burdens
To weigh down; oppress

Psalms 38: 4
Psalms 42: 6
Psalms 55: 22
Psalms 68: 19
Psalms 81: 6
Isaiah 9: 4
Isaiah 10: 27
Matthew 23
Luke 17:1-4
John 8:4-11
Romans 1.28-30
Romans 14:13
Romans 14:15-21 (Will not offend a brother)
Romans 15:1-3 (strong ought to bear)
1 Corinthians 1:10-16
1 Corinthians 3:10-12
2 Corinthians 12.15-16[though the more abundantly I love
    you, the less I be loved]
Galatians 6.2
1 Thessalonians 4.6
1 Peter 5.7
2 Peter 2.19

C

Comfort
To soothe in time of affliction or distress

Romans 15:1-3 (strong ought to bear)
2 Corinthians 1:4
2 Corinthians 2:7
Philippians 2:1
1 Thessalonians 3:2, 7
1 Thessalonians 4:18
1 Thessalonians 5:11,14
James 5.16
1 John 5:16

Compassion
Deep awareness of the suffering of another coupled with the wish to relieve it

Matthew 9:36
Matthew 14:14
Matthew 15:32
Matthew 18:27
Matthew 18:33
Matthew 20:34
Mark 1:4
Mark 6:34
Luke 7:13
Luke 10:33 (Good Samaritans Society)
Luke 15:20
Acts 9:33
Romans 9:15
James 3:17
1 Peter 3:8-9
1 John 3:17

Conceited (Arrogant)
A favorable and especially unduly high opinion of one's
own abilities or worth.

Romans 11:20
Galatians 5:26
1 Corinthians 4:18, 19
1 Corinthians 5:2
1 Corinthians 13:5
2 Corinthians 11:20
1 Timothy 6:17
2 Timothy 3:2
Titus 1:7
1 Peter 5:3
Jude 1:16

Condemn
To pronounce judgment against

Matthews 7:1-2
Matthews 12:7
Matthews 23:14
Luke 6:37 *
Luke 18:10-14
Luke 19:22
John 3:17
John 8:10, 11, 15
Romans 2:1-3
Galatians 6:1-4
James 5:6

Conspire

To plan together secretly to commit an illegal or wrongful act or accomplish a legal purpose through illegal action.

Matthews 26:14
Acts 5:9
Acts 9:23
Acts 23:13, 14
Acts 23:30

Contention

The act or an instance of striving in controversy or debate.

Matthew 5:21-25 (angry gift)
Matthew 5:43-47
Matthew 7:1-5
Matthew 20.26
Matthew 23
Mark 12*38
Luke 17:1-4
John 2:16
John 8:4-11
Acts 4:1, 2
Acts 11:1-3
Acts 13:50
Acts 14:2
Romans 1.28-30
Romans 11:20
Romans 14:15-21 (Will not offend a brother)
1 Corinthians 1:10-16
1 Corinthians 3:3-5
1 Corinthians 4.6
1 Corinthians 8:9
2 Corinthians 4:2
Philippians 1:16

Philippians 2:3, 14
Colossians 3:13
1 Thessalonians 4.6
1 Thessalonians 5:12-15
2 Thessalonians 3:6, 11
2 Thessalonians 3:13-15 (Note the brother but do not look
    at him like an enemy)
1 Timothy 1:5-7 (charity with pure heart)
1 Timothy 1:19 (shipwreck)
1 Timothy 3:3
2 Timothy 4:2
Titus 3:3
Titus 3:10,11
James 4.11
James 4.16
James 5.9
1 Peter 2.1
1 Peter 2.23
1 Peter 3.8-11
2 Peter 3.3
Jude 1:16

Covetousness
Marked by extreme desire to acquire or possess:

2 Samuel 15:2
Matthew 6:6
Matthew 10.8
Matthew 13.58
Matthew 20.26
Luke 12:15
John 8:4-11
Romans 1.28-30
Romans 7.7
1 Corinthians 3:3-5
1 Corinthians 6:10

1 Corinthians 10.33
Ephesians 5:3, 5
Philippians 2:3, 14
Colossians 3:5 (idolatry)
Hebrews 13.5
James 3.14-16
James 4.16
2 Peter 2.3
2 Peter 2.14

Crafty
Skilled in or marked by underhandedness, deviousness, or
    deception.

Genesis 3:1
Genesis 27:35
2 Samuel 13:3-7 (what it does
2 Samuel 15:2
Job 5:12 (cannot perform their enterprise)
Job 5:15
Proverbs7:10
Daniel 8:23-25[prosper don't mean blessed] / read translation
Matthew 26:4
Acts 13:10-11 [child of devil]
Mark 14*1
Luke 20:23 [perceive craftiness]
John 2:16
Acts 13:6-7
Acts 19:25
1 Corinthians 3:19
2 Corinthians 4.2 [nor handling the word of God deceitfully]
2 Corinthians 11:3
2 Corinthians 12.15-16[though the more abundantly I love
    you, the less I am loved]
2 Corinthians 12.14-21 [wow]
Ephesians 4:14 **[Cunning (skillful)**

Criticize
To judge the merits and faults of; analyze and evaluate

Matthew 7:1-2
Luke 18:10-14
Romans 9:20
Romans 14:1,3,10,13*, 16
James 4:11

Curse
An appeal or prayer for evil or misfortune to befall someone or something

Romans 12:14
1 Corinthians 3:10-12
James 3.9-12
2 Peter 3.3
Jude 1:16

D

Debate
To engage in argument by discussing opposing points.

Isaiah 58:4
Acts 6:9
Acts 11:18
Acts 13:13
Acts 14:23
Acts 15:7, 37-39
Romans 1:29

Deceit
The act or practice of deceiving; deception

2 Samuel 15:2
Job 27:4
Psalms 101:7
Jeremiah 9:8
Jeremiah 14:14
Jeremiah 23:26
Matthew 15.11
Matthew 24:11, 24
Matthew 26:14-15
Mark 7:22
John 2:16
John 8:4-11
Acts 13:10
Romans 1:29
Romans 3:13
Romans 3:13-14
Romans 12:9-10
Colossians 2:8
1 Thessalonians 2:3
1 Thessalonians 4.6

2 Thessalonians 2:3
1 Timothy 4:2
Titus 3:10, 11
1 John 2:26
1 John 3:

Devour
To destroy, consume, or waste

Matthew 5:21-25 (angry gift)
Matthew 10.36
Matthew 13.58
Matthew 20.26
Matthew 23
John 8:4-11
Romans 12:9-10
Romans 14:13
Romans 14:15-21 (Will not offend a brother)
1 Corinthians 1:10-16
1 Corinthians 4.6
1 Corinthians 11:18-19
Galatians 5.6
Galatians 5.15
Philippians 2:14
Colossians 3:9 (lie not one to another)
1 Thessalonians 4.6
2 Thessalonians 3:6,11
2 Thessalonians 3:13-15
James 3.14-16
2 Peter 2.11-12
2 Peter 2.19
1 John 3.14-16

Disagreement
A conflict or difference of opinion

Matthew 5:43-47
Matthew 6.12,14,15
Matthew 18:15-17
Luke 17:1-4
Romans 1.28-30
Romans 14:13
1 Corinthians 3:3-5
1 Corinthians 4.6
1 Corinthians 11:18-19
Philippians 2:14
Philippians 4:8
1 Corinthians 1:10-16
Colossians 3:13
1 Thessalonians 5:12-14
2 Thessalonians 3:6, 11
2 Thessalonians 3:13-15 (Note the brother but do not look at him like an enemy)
James 4.11
1 Peter 4.9
2 Peter 3.3

Disciples
One who embraces and assists in spreading the teachings of another

Matthew 5:43-47
Matthew 6.12,14,15
Matthew 7:15-20
Matthew 12:49-50
Matthew 15.11
Matthew 20.26
Matthew 26.50
Mark 3:34

Mark 5:18 [go to your family]
Luke 6.27-28
John 13.34-35(disciples)
John 15.13
Acts 13:1-3
Romans 12:9-10
Romans 12:18 (live peaceably)
1 Corinthians 3:3-5
1 Corinthians 3:10-12
1 Corinthians 13
1 Corinthians 16:14 (All things done in Love)
2 Corinthians 12.15-16 [though the more abundantly I love
    you, the less I be loved]
Philemon 1:14
Hebrews 13.17
1 John 4:7-13
3 John 3:9-10

Division (Cause It)
Disunion; difference in opinion or feeling; discord;
    variance; alienation.

2 Samuel 15:2
Matthew 5:21-25 (angry gift)
Matthews. 13.58
Matthew20.26
Acts 14:2-5
Romans 12:9-10
Romans 14:13
Romans 14:15-21 (Will not offend a brother)
Romans 16:17-18
1 Corinthians 1:10-16
1 Corinthians 3:3-5
1 Corinthians 11:18-19
Ephesians 5:6-7
Ephesians 5:11-12

Philippians 2:14
Philippians 3:2, 6, 18-19
Colossians 3:9 (lie not one to another)
Colossians 3:13
1 Thessalonians 5:12-14
2 Thessalonians 3:6, 11
2 Thessalonians 3:13-15 (Note the brother but do not look at him like an enemy)
1 Timothy 6:3-5
2 Timothy 3:2-4
2 Timothy 4:2
Titus 1:10-11 (filthy lucre)
Titus 3:10,11
James 4.11
James 4.16
James 5.9
2 Peter 2.19

E

Edifying
To instruct especially so as to encourage intellectual, moral, or spiritual improvement

Ecclesiastes 4:9
John 13.34-35(disciples)
Acts 9:25
Romans 12:16
Romans 14:15-21 (Will not offend a brother)
Romans 15:1-3 (strong ought to bear)
2 Corinthians 12.15-16 [though the more abundantly I love you, the less I am loved]
Ephesians 4:29
Philippians 2:4
Colossians 1:4
Colossians 3:11
1 Thessalonians 5:12-15
Titus 3:2 (Speak evil of no man)
Philemon 1:7
Hebrews 10.25
1 Peter 2.1
3 John 1:2-8

Encourage
To inspire with hope, courage, or confidence; hearten.

2 Corinthians 1:4
2 Corinthians 2:7
Ephesians 6:22
Colossians 4:8
1 Thessalonians 3:2
1 Thessalonians 4:18
1 Thessalonians 5:11,14
2 Thessalonians 2:17

1 Timothy 1:16
Hebrews 3:13
1 Peter 2:14

Enemies
One who feels hatred toward, intends injury to, or opposes
    the interests of another; a foe

2 Samuel 1:2 - 14, 17
Matthews 5:44
Luke 6:27, 35

Envying
A feeling of discontent and resentment aroused by and in
    conjunction with desire for the possessions or qualities
    of another.

Matthew 6:6
Mark 15:10
John 9:34
Acts 13:45
Romans 1.28-30
Romans 13:13
1 Corinthians 1:10-16
1 Corinthians 3:3-5
1 Corinthians 13.4
Galatians 5.26
Ephesians 4:31
Philippians 1:15 **
Philippians 2:3
1 Thessalonians 4.6
James 3.14-16
James 4.5
James 5.9
1 Peter 2.1
Jude 1:16

Evil Speaking
Causing ruin, injury, or pain; harmful

Ephesus 4:31
Titus 3:2
James 4:11
1 Peter 2:1
1 Peter 3:10

Esteem Higher
To regard with respect; prize

Matthew 5:21-25 (angry gift)
1 Corinthians 10.33
Romans 12:16
Romans 15:1-3 (strong ought to bear)
Philippians 2:3, 4
1 Thessalonians 5:12-14

Exhort
Acts 11:23
Acts 27:22
Romans 12:8
2 Corinthians 9:5
1 Thessalonians 2:11
1 Thessalonians 4:1
1 Thessalonians 5:11
2 Thessalonians 3:12
1 Timothy 2:1
1 Timothy 4:13
2 Timothy 4:2
Titus 1:9
Titus 2:6
Hebrews 3:13 ***
Hebrews 13:22
Jude 3

F

Family
All the members of a household under one roof.

Matthew12.49-50
Mark 5:18 [go to your family]
Ephesians 6:1-4
Colossians 3:20-21
1 Timothy 3:4,5
1 Timothy 5:8
Titus 1:6
1 Peter 3

Fear
A feeling of agitation and anxiety caused by the presence or
    imminence of danger

1 John 4:18

Fighting
To attempt to harm or gain power over an adversary by
    blows or with weapons

Matthew 5:43-47
Acts 7:26
Romans 12:18 (live peaceably)
Romans 14:13
1 Corinthians 1:10-16
2 Corinthians 7:5
Galatians 5.15, 16
Colossians 3:9 (lie not one to another)
2 Thessalonians 3:13-15 (Note the brother but do not look
    at him like an enemy)
2 Timothy 2:24

Filthy Lucre
Shameful gain

Acts 3:6
Acts 4:34
Acts 5
Acts 8:19
Acts 15:19
1 Timothy 3:3
1 Timothy 3:8
1 Timothy 6:10
Titus 1:7-11
1 Peter 5:2
2 Peter 2:7

Forbear
To desist from; cease

Matthew 6.12,14,15
Luke 6.27-28
John 5:42
John 8:4-11
Romans 14:15-21 (Will not offend a brother)
1 Corinthians 13
Ephesians 4.2
Ephesians 4:15, 32
Colossians 3:13
Titus 3:2 (Speak evil of no man)
Hebrews 13.1(let brotherly love cont)
1 Peter 3.4
1 John 3.17
1 John 4:7-13

Forgive
To excuse for a fault or an offense; pardon

Proverbs 19.11
Matthew 6.12,14,15
Matthew 9.5,6
Matthew 18.21-22
Mark 11:25-26
Matthew 18.21-35 (parable)
Matthew 18.35 don't forgive no heaven
Luke 5.24 (forgive before healing)
Luke 6.37
Luke 17.3,4
Luke 23.34
John 5:42
John 8:4-11
Romans 15:1-3 (strong ought to bear)
Ephesians 4:32
Colossians 3:13
Philemon 1:16
James 2.13

Fraud
A deception deliberately practiced in order to secure unfair
    or unlawful gain

1 Thessalonians 2:3
James 5:4

Fruit Bad
Matthew7:1-5
Matthew15.11
Mark 7:20-23
John 8:4-11
Galatians 5.20, 21
Ephesians 4:14

Ephesians 4:31
Ephesians 5:11-12
Philippians 2:14
Colossians 3:5, 8, 9(Lie)
2 Timothy 4:2
Titus 3:10, 11
2 Peter 2.19

Fruit Good
Matthew 5:43-47
Matthew 7:1-5
Matthew 7:15-20
Matthew 12.33
Galatians 5.6
Galatians 5.22
Galatians 6.10
Ephesians 2.10
Ephesians 4:29, 32
Ephesians 5:2, 25, 28, 33 (Husbands must do)
Philippians 2:2
Colossians 1:4
Colossians 2:2, 19 (Knitted in Love)
Colossians 3:19 (Husbands love)
James 3.17

G

Gentle

Considerate or kindly in disposition; amiable and tender.

Colossians 3:12-13
1 Thessalonians 2:7
1 Timothy 3:3
2 Timothy 2:24
Titus 3:2
James 1:21
James 3:17
1 Peter 3:4

God Loves-We Should Love

Matthew 5:43-47
Matthew15.11
Matthew19.19
John 3:16
John 5:42
Galatians 5.6
1 Corinthians 4:20-21
1 Corinthians 13
2 Corinthians 12.15-16 [though the more abundantly I love
   you, the less I be loved]
1 John 4:7-13
1 John 4:16-17

Good

Being positive or desirable in nature; not bad or poor: *a*
good experience

Galatians 6.10
1 Peter 2:12, 14
Romans 12:9
Romans 13:3

1 Timothy 5:10, 25
Titus 2:7
1 John 4:7-13
1 John 5:16

Greed
An excessive desire to acquire or possess more than what one
    needs or deserves, especially with respect to material
    wealth

2 Samuel 15:2
Mark 7:21-22
Luke 11:39
Luke 12:15
Acts 5
Romans 1:29
1 Corinthians 5:10-11
1 Corinthians 6:9-10
1 Corinthians 10:24
Ephesians 4:9
Ephesians 4:19
Ephesians 5:3, 5
Colossians 3:5
1 Thessalonians 2:5
1 Timothy 3:3, 8
2 Timothy 3:2
Titus 1:7
Hebrews 13:5
2 Peter 1:4
2 Peter 2:14
2 Peter 2:3
1 John 2:16
Jude 1:11

Grudge
To be reluctant to give or admit

Matthew 5:21-25 (angry gift)
Matthew 7:1-5
Romans 14:13
1 Corinthians 1:10-16
1 Corinthians 8:9
2 Corinthians 12.15-16 [though the more abundantly I love
   you, the less I be loved]
James 5.9
1 Peter 4.9
2 Peter 3.3
Jude 1:16

Guile
Treacherous cunning; skillful deceit

Psalms 32:2
Psalms 34:13
Matthew 26:14-16
John 1:475
John 8:4-11
2 Corinthians 12:16
2 Corinthians 12.15-16 [though the more abundantly I love
   you, the less I am loved]
1 Thessalonians 2:3
2 Timothy 4:2
1 Peter 2:1
1 Peter 2:22
1 Peter 3:10
Revelations 14:5

H

Hate
To feel hostility or animosity toward

Matthew 5.22
Matthew 5:43-47
Matthew13.58
Matthew15.11
Luke 6.27-28
Romans 1.28-30
Titus 3:3
1 John 2.9,11
1 John 3.14-16
1 John 4:7-13
1 John 4:20, 21

Haughty
Scornfully and condescendingly proud

Matthews 23:12
Luke 1:51
Romans 12:16 *
1 Corinthians 13:4
James 4:6

Honest
Not deceptive or fraudulent.
Characterized by truth; not false: honest reporting. Sincere;
    frank

Genesis 42:33
1 Samuel 29:6
Proverbs 31:11
Luke 8:15:17
John 4

John 7:24
Acts 6:3
Romans 12:17
2 Corinthians 6:7-8
2 Corinthians 8:21 *
2 Corinthians 13:7
Philippians 4:8
Titus 3:14
Hebrews 10:22

Hospitality
Cordial and generous reception of or disposition toward
   guests

Matthew 5:13 (salt)
Matthew10.8
Romans 12:13
Romans 14:15-21 (Will not offend a brother)
Acts 16:15
1 Corinthians 10.24

Household of Faith
John 15.13
Romans 12:16
Galatians 6.14
1 Thessalonians 5:12-14
Titus 3:2 (Speak evil of no man)
Hebrews 10.23-24
Hebrews 13.17
James 5.16
John 13.34-35(disciples)
1 John 4:7-13
2 John 1:15-16

Humble

Marked by meekness or modesty in behavior, attitude, or spirit; not arrogant or prideful

Proverbs 3:34
Matthews 5:3
Matthews 11:29
Matthews 18:4
Matthews 23:12
Luke 18:10-14
Romans 12:16
Philippians 2:3-5
James 1:21
James 4:6,10
1 Peter 5:5, 6 *

Hypocrites

The practice of professing beliefs, feelings, or virtues that one does not hold or possess; falseness.

Matthew 6:2, 5, 16
Matthew 7:5
Matthew 15:7
Matthew 16:3
Matthew 22:18
Matthew 23:13, 14,15,23,25,27,28,29
Matthew 24:51
Mark 7:6
Mark 12:15
Luke 6:42
Luke 11:44
Luke 12:1, 56
Luke 13:15
Galatians 2:13
1 Timothy 4:2
James 3:17
1 Peter 2:1

I

Innocent:
Matthews 10:16
Acts 28:18
Romans 16:19
2 Corthians 6:6
Philippians 2:15
1 Peter 3:18

J

Jealousy
Fearful or wary of being supplanted; apprehensive of losing
    affection or position

Matthew 15.11
Acts 5:17
Acts 13:45
Acts 17:5
Romans 1:29
Romans 13:13
1 Corinthians 3:3
1 Corinthians 13:4
2 Corinthians 12.15-16 [though the more abundantly I love
    you, the less I am loved]
2 Corinthians 12.20
Galatians 5:20
1 Timothy 6:4
Titus 3:3
James 3:14, 16
1 Peter 2:1

Judgment
To form an opinion or estimation of after careful
    consideration

Matthew 7:1-5
Matthew 18:21-35
Luke 6:37, 40-43 [acquit and forgive and °release]
Luke 12:14
Luke 19:22
John 7:24
John 8:4-11, 15
John 12:47
Acts 23:3

Romans 2:1, 3-5
Romans 14:13
Romans 14:10
1 Corinthians 4:20-21
1 Corinthians 6:5
1 Corinthians 11:31
Galatians 5.21
Philippians 1:9,
James 4:11
James 5.9

K

Keep Your Word
1 John 2.5

Kindness
An instance of kind behavior

Luke 1:50, 72, 78
John 1:14
Acts 4:33
Acts 27:3
Acts 28:2
Romans 2:4
Romans 11:22
1 Corinthians 7:3
1 Corinthians 13.4
2 Corinthians 6:6
2 Corinthians 1:12
2 Corinthians 6:1, 6
2 Corinthians 8:9
2 Corinthians 9:9, 10
2 Corinthians 12:9
Galatians 5:22
Ephesus 2:7
Colossians 3:12
1 Thessalonians 5:15
2 Timothy 1:16
Titus 3:4
Hebrews 13:16
2 Peter 1:7

Knowledge and Judgment
John 8:4-11
1 Corinthians 4:20-21
Philippians 1:9
Colossians 4:6 (speech with salt)
1 John 4:7-13
1 John 4:20, 21

L

Love
A deep, tender, ineffable feeling of affection and solicitude toward a person, such as that arising from kinship, recognition of attractive qualities, or a sense of underlying oneness.

Love in Action
Matthew 5:13, 16, 20 (salt)
Matthew 5:21-25 (angry gift
Matthew 5:43-47
Matthew 19.19
Matthew 22:34-40
Mark 12:31-33
Luke 6.27-28
Luke 10.25-28
John 3:16
John 5:42
John 8:31
John 13.34-35(disciples)
John 14.15
John 15.12,13,17
John 17.26**
Romans 12:9-10
Romans 12:18 (live peaceably)
Romans 13:8-10
Romans 14:15-21 (Will not offend a brother)
Romans 15:14
1 Corinthians 13
1 Corinthians 16:14 (All things done in Love)
Galatians 5.6
Galatians 5.14
Galatians 6.2
Philippians 2:4
Colossians 1:4 (all the saints)

Colossians 3:14 (perfect ness)
1 Thessalonians 4:9
1 Thessalonians 5:12-14
1 Timothy 1:5-7 (charity w/pure heart)
2 Timothy 1:7
Titus 3:2
Philemon 1:5
Hebrews 10.23-24 (Proverbs provoke to Love)
Hebrews 13.1(let brotherly love cont)
James 2.8
James 3.17
James 5.13-14
1 Peter 1.22
1 Peter 2.17
1 Peter 3.8-11
1 Peter 4.8
1 John 3.17
1 John 4:7-13
1 John 4:16-17
1 John 4:20, 21
1 John 5:2
2 John 1:15-16

Love in Deed
Matthew 5:43-47
Matthew 7:15-20
Matthew 24:46
Matthew 25:34
Mark 7.15
Mark 12:31
Luke 10.25-28
Luke 10:30
John 5:42
Romans 14:15-21 (Will not offend a brother)
1 Corinthians 1:10-16
1 Corinthians 10.33

1 Corinthians 12.26
1 Corinthians 13
1 Corinthians 16:14 (All things done in Love)
2 Corinthians 12.15-16[though the more abundantly I love you, the less I am loved]
Philippians 2:4
Colossians 4:6 (speech with salt)
1 Thessalonians 1.3
1 Timothy 1:5-7 (charity with pure heart)
Hebrews 10.23-24
1 John 2.5
1 John 3.17
1 John 3:18*
1 John 4:7-13
2 John 1:15-16

Love Faith
1 Corinthians 13:7
Galatians 5.6
Ephesians 6:23
1 Timothy 1:14
Hebrews 10.23-24

Love of God
Matthew 5:43-47
Luke 6.27-28
Luke 10.25-28
John 5:42
John 8:4-11
1 Corinthians 4:20-21
1 Corinthians 13
1 Corinthians 16:14 (All things done in Love)
2 Corinthians 13:11
Galatians 5.6
Ephesians 2.4,5,6
Ephesians 3.17-20

Colossians 2:2, 19 (Knitted in Love)
John 17.26
1 Thessalonians 4:9
1 John 3.17
1 John 4:7-13
1 John 4:16-17

Love God Hate Man
Matthew 5:43-47
Luke 6.27-28
John 5:42
1 John 4:7-13
1 John 4:16-17, 20-21
2 John 1:15-16

Love One Another (Royal Law)
Matthew 5:13, 16, 20(salt)
Matthew 5:43-47
Matthews 19:19
Matthew 22:34-40 **
Mark 12:30-34
Luke 6:27-28. 32-38
Luke 10.25-28
Romans 12:10
Romans 13:8-10
Romans 14:15-21 (Will not offend a brother)
1 Corinthians 16:14 (All things done in Love)
Galatians 5.6
James 2.8
1 Peter 1.22
John 13.34-35(disciples)
1 John 4:20, 21

Power of Love
Romans 14:15-21 (Will not offend a brother)
Romans 15:1-3 (strong ought to bear)

Romans 15:7 (Receive One another)
1 Corinthians 13
Galatians 5.6
Ephesians 1.4
Ephesians 2.4,5,6,10
Ephesians 3.17-20
Ephesians 4.12,13
Ephesians 4:15
Philippians 3:13, 16
Colossians 1:8 (In the spirit)
Colossians 1:10 (Every good work)
1 Timothy 1:5-7 (charity with pure heart)
Hebrews 13.1(let brotherly love cont)
James 5.16
1 John 2.10
1 John 3.14
1 John 4:7-13
1 John 4:16-17
1 John 4:18
1 John 4:20, 21

Love Walk
Matthew 5:43-47
John 3:16
Romans 14:15-21 (Will not offend a brother)
1 Corinthians 16:14 (All things done in Love)
Ephesians 4:25
Ephesians 5:2
1 Thessalonians 5:12-14
1 Peter 1.22
1 John 4:16-17
1 John 4:20, 21

Lying

A false statement deliberately presented as being true; a falsehood.

Acts 5:3
Ephesus 4:25
Colossians 3:9
James 3:14

M

Maliciousness
Having the nature of or resulting from malice; deliberately
   harmful; spiteful

Matthew 5:43-47
Matthew 9:4
Luke 11:39
Romans 14:15-21 (Will not offend a brother)
1 Corinthians 3:3-5
1 Corinthians 5:8
Ephesus 4:31
Colossians 3:8
1 Thessalonians 4.6
Titus 3:3
Titus 3:10, 11
1 Peter 2:1
1 Peter 2.16
2 Peter 2.19
2 Peter 3.3
Jude 1:16

Marriage
Matthew 5:43-47
Matthew 19.4
Mark 10:6, 7
Luke 16:18
Romans 15:1-3 (strong ought to bear)
1 Corinthians 7
1 Corinthians 11.11,12
1 Corinthians 10.24
Ephesians 5:22-25, 28,29,31,33
Colossians 3:18-19

Meek
Showing patience and humility; gentle

Matthew 5:5
Matthew 11:29
Mark 10.45
1 Corinthians 4:20-21
1 Peter 3.4 (meek & quiet)

Mercy
A disposition to be kind and forgiving

Matthew 5:7
Matthew 7:1-5
Matthew 10.8
John 8:4-11
1 Corinthians 4:20-21
Philippians 2:1
Colossians 3:12
James 2.15-17
1 John 3.17

Murmurings
To utter complaints in a low, half-articulated voice; to feel or express dissatisfaction or discontent

John 6:43
Romans 12:16
1 Corinthians 3:10-12
Philippians 2:14
James 5.9

N

Neighbor
A person, place, or thing adjacent to or located near another.

Matthew 5.5
Matthew 5:21-25 (angry gift)
Matthew 5:43-47
Matthew 12:49.50
Matthew 22:34-40
Matthew 19.19
Matthew 23.39
Mark 5:18 [go to your family]
Mark 12.31,33
Luke 8.38
Luke 10.5, 27
John 8:4-11
John 15.13
Romans 12:9-10
Romans 12:18 (live peaceably)
Romans 13:8-10
Romans 14:13
Romans 15:1-3 (strong ought to bear)
Romans 15:7 (Receive One another),
1 Corinthians 10.24
1 Corinthians 12.25
2 Corinthians 8:21
2 Corinthians 11:22
Ephesians 4:25
Titus 3:2 (Speak evil of no man)
Hebrews 13.1(let brotherly love cont)
James 2
James 2.8
James 2.15-17
James 5.20
1 Peter 1.22

1 Peter 2.17
1 Peter 3.8-11
1 Peter 4.8
1 John 2.10
1 John 3.14-17
1 John 4:7-13
1 John 4:16-17
1 John 4:20, 21
1 John 5:2
1 John 5:16
2 John 1:15-16

O

Offence

The act of offending in any sense; esp., a crime or a sin, an affront or an injury.

Matthew 5:21-25 (angry gift)
Matthew 13.58
Matthew 15.11
Matthew 16:23
Matthew 18.9
Mark 9:45
Luke 17:1-4
John 5:42
John 9:34
Acts 6:11
Romans 1.28-30
Romans 4:25 (Delivered from offence)
Romans 14:13
Romans 14:15-21 (Will not offend a brother)
2 Corinthians 6:3
Ephesians 1:10
Philippians 1.10
Philippians 2:15
Colossians 3:9 (lie not one to another)
Colossians 3:13
1 Thessalonians 5:12-14
2 Thessalonians 3:6, 11
James 3.2
James 5.9
1 Peter 2.23
1 Peter 4.9
2 Peter 3.3

Ordination
The ceremony of consecration to the ministry

Acts 6:5
Acts 13:1-3
Acts 14:23

P

Partiality
Favorable prejudice or bias

Matthew6.6
Matthew18
Matthew22.6
James 2
James 2.9
James 3.17
John 13.34-35(disciples)

Peace
Freedom from quarrels and disagreement; harmonious relations

Luke 10:5
John 14:27
Romans 12:18
1 Corinthians 14:33
2 Corinthians 13:11
Ephesians 6:23
Colossians 3:15
1 Thessalonians 5:13
Hebrews 12:14
James 3:17-18
1 Peter 3:11
Jude 1:2

Perfect ness
Lacking nothing essential to the whole

Matthew5:43-47
1 Corinthians 1:10-16
Colossians 3:14
1 Timothy 1:5-7 (charity with pure heart)

Hebrews 10.23-24 (Proverbs provoke to Love)
James 3.2
James 3.17
1 John 4:7-13
1 John 4:16-17
1 John 4:18

Pretence (false)

The act of holding out, to others something false or feigned; presentation of what is deceptive ; deception by showing what is unreal and concealing what is real

Matthew 7:1-5
Matthew 23
Romans 1.28-30
1 Corinthians 3:10-12
Philippians 1:18
Philippians 2:15
Philippians 3:2
2 Timothy 4:2
2 Peter 2.19

Pride

Pleasure or satisfaction taken in an achievement, possession, or association

Matthews 23:12
Mark 7:22
Luke 12:16-21
Acts 12:22-23
Romans 11:18
1 Corinthians 4:6
1 Corinthians 13:5
Ephesians 2:9
Philippians 3:3
1 Timothy 3:6

1 Timothy 6:4
James 3:14
1 Peter 5:5
1 John 2:16

Pure Heart
Matthews 5:8
1 Timothy 1:5-7
2 Timothy 2:22
Titus 1:15
1 Peter 1:22

Q

Quarrelsome
An angry dispute; an altercation

Acts 7:26
Romans 1:29
Romans 13:13
1 Corinthians 6:5
1 Corinthians 11:16
2 Corinthians 12:20
Ephesians 4:31
Colossians 3:13
Philippians 1:16
1 Timothy 2:8
1 Timothy 3:3
1 Timothy 6:4
2 Timothy 2:23-24
James 4:1

R

Racism
The belief that race accounts for differences in human
character or ability and that a particular race is superior
to others

Matthew 7:1-5
Matthew 8:8-11
Matthew13.58
Matthew15.11
Matthew22.6
John 3:16
John 5:42
Acts 2:8
Acts 6
Acts 10:14, 28, 34, 45
Acts 11:1-3
Acts 13:48
Acts 15:19
Romans 10:12-13
1 Corinthians 1:10-16
1 Corinthians 3:3-5
1 Corinthians 12.25
Galatians 2:11
Galatians 3.28
Ephesians 1.10
Ephesians 2.19,22
Ephesians 3.6, 9
Ephesians 4.3,4,6,12,25
Ephesians 5:30
Philippians 2:2
Philippians 3:2
Philippians 4:3
Colossians 1:4
Colossians 2:2, 19 (Knitted in Love)

Colossians 3:11
Hebrews 13.1(let brotherly love cont)
James 2
James 2.9
1 Peter 2.23
John 13.34-35(disciples)
1 John 2.9,11
1 John 3.14-16
1 John 4:20, 21

Scorners
Contempt or disdain felt toward a person or object
considered despicable or unworthy

Matthew 18:10
Luke 18:9
Acts 13:41
Galatians 4:14
Galatians 6:7
2 Peter 2:10

Selfish
Caring supremely or unduly for one's self; regarding one's
own comfort, advantage, etc., in disregard, or at the
expense, of those of others.

Matthew14:14-15
Matthew20.26
Luke 6:35
Luke 12:20
John 8:4-11
1 Corinthians 10.24
1 Corinthians 13.5
2 Corinthians 12.20
Galatians 5:13, 2
Phil 2.3
James 3.14-16
James 4:3

Serving
To be a servant to.

Matthew10.8
Matthew20.26

John 10
John 13:12
Romans 15:1-3 (strong ought to bear)
1 Corinthians 3:10-12
1 Corinthians 9:19
1 Corinthians 16:14 (All things done in Love)
Galatians 5.13
Philippians 2:4, 7, 8
Hebrews 13.17
James 2.15-17
1 Peter 2.16

Speak the Truth
Matthew15.11
Ephesians 4:15, 25
Philippians 1:9
Colossians 3:13
Colossians 4:6 (speech with salt)
2 Thessalonians 2:10
1 John 3:18
Jude 1:16

Spiritual Dead
1 John 3:14

Strife (Competition)
Heated, often violent dissension; bitter conflict.

Mark 10:35-43
Luke 22:24
Acts 1:26
Romans 13:13
1 Corinthians 3:3
2 Corinthians 10:12 (Comparing)
2 Corinthians 12:13
Galatians 5:15, 26

Galatians 6:4(Comparing)
Philippians 1:15
Philippians 2:3
1 Timothy 6:4
2 Timothy 2:23
James 3:14, 16
James 4:1

Submit
To yield or surrender (oneself) to the will or authority of
another.

Matthew20.26
1 Corinthians 16:16
Ephesians 5:21
Philippians 2:4
Colossians 3:12, 13
Hebrews 13.17
1 Peter 2.16

T

Tongue
James 3.3-8
James 3.9-12
1 Peter 3.8-11
1 John 3:18*

Truth
Conformity to fact or actuality.
A statement proven to be or accepted as true.
Sincerity; integrity.

John 4:23-24
John 8:32, 44
John 14:17
John16:7 (Speak the truth even with bad news)
John 17:17
1 Corinthians 13:6
2 Corinthians 4:2
2 Corinthians 13:8
Ephesians 4:15, 25 *
Ephesians 5:9
Ephesians 6:14
James 3:14
1 John 1:8
1 John3: 18
3 John 1:4

U

Unity
The state or quality of being one; singleness

Acts 1:14
Acts 2:44
Acts 4:32
Romans 12:4-6
1 Corinthians 3
1 Corinthians 12
1 Corinthians 16:14 (All things done in Love)
2 Corinthians 11:22
2 Corinthians 13:11
Ephesians 2:14
Ephesians 4:3, 13
Philippians 2:2
Philippians 3:15, 16
Colossians 2:2, 19 (Knitted in Love)
Colossians 3:11
Hebrews 10.25
Hebrews 13.1(let brotherly love cont)
1 Thessalonians 5:12-14
1 Peter 1.22
1 Peter 3.8-11
John 13.34-35(disciples)
1 John 4:7-13

Unselfishness
The quality of not putting yourself first but being willing to
    give your time, money, or effort etc. for others

1 Corinthians 10:24
1 Corinthians 10:33
Ephesians 4:2
Philippians 2:4
Philippians 4:5

V

Vengeance
Infliction of punishment in return for a wrong committed; retribution.

Genesis 50:19
Luke 6:35
Luke 14:14
Luke 18:7
Romans 12:17.18, 19 21
1 Thessalonians 5:15

NOTES

NOTES:

NOTES:

NOTES:

Printed in the United States
117775LV00001B/151-159/P